WALKING THROUGH THE VALLEY OF

DEPRESSION AND GRIEF

CREDITS
Project Manager: Dr. Bob Marshall
Assistants: Rochelle Chalifoux and Kristi Wertz
Transcription: Cyndilu Marshall
Page Design and Layout: Linda Stubblefield
Proofreading: Rena Fish, Laurie Whitehouse

To order additional books by Dr. Jack Schaap,
please contact:
HYLES PUBLICATIONS
523 Sibley Street
Hammond, Indiana 46320
www.hylespublications.com
e-mail: info@hylespublications.com

WALKING THROUGH THE VALLEY OF

DEPRESSION AND GRIEF

Dr. Jack Schaap
Pastor of First Baptist Church
Hammond, Indiana

HYLES PUBLICATIONS | HAMMOND, INDIANA

I OWE A GREAT *debt of gratitude to my editorial advisor, Mrs. Linda Stubblefield, who has labored long and hard to make my thoughts and heart clear to readers. Since 1977, Mrs. Stubblefield has been an employee of Christian Womanhood in various capacities. She presently serves there as the assistant editor. She has worked in the bus ministry for 20 years. She is married to David Stubblefield, and they are the parents of two adult daughters.*

DEDICATION

I KNOW OF NO one who has brought more joy to those caught in the web of depression and grief than Maxine Jeffries. "Max" is a joy-giver. Maxine helped to start our ministry to the deaf and the hard of hearing over 40 years ago. She also is the director of our shut-in ministry, bringing sunshine and happiness to those in nursing homes or those unable to get out of their own homes.

Maxine also assists our church families during the loss of a loved one. Again and again Maxine has been the first person to open the door of hope when circumstances slammed it shut.

Along with all of those duties, Maxine helps her pastor send flowers and words of encouragement to church members and others in their times of grief and sadness.

On behalf of a grateful church, thank you, Maxine, from the bottom of my heart.

"MOST OF THE GRAND TRUTHS OF GOD HAVE TO BE LEARNED BY TROUBLE; THEY MUST BE BURNED INTO US BY THE HOT IRON OF AFFLICTION, OTHERWISE WE SHALL NOT TRULY RECEIVE THEM."

—CHARLES SPURGEON

TABLE OF CONTENTS

Chapter One
  I'm Not Gonna Give Up on Me .9

Chapter Two
  Riding My Failure to Success .23

Chapter Three
  How Do I Walk Throught the Valley? 35

Chapter Four
  Perfecting Your Fears 49

Chapter Five
  Why Can't I Get Up When I Fall? 61

Chapter Six
  Where Was God in the Day of My Trouble? 69

Chapter Seven
  Feeling at Home in the Shadows 79

Chapter Eight
  I'll Use My Burden to Carry Yours 91

Chapter Nine
  Blessed Are Those Who Get the Wind Knocked
    out of Them 97

Chapter Ten
   The Trial of Bitter Water 105

Chapter Eleven
   If You Want to Be an Overcomer, You Must
      Learn to Overcome 113

Chapter Twelve
   I Will Leave Off My Heaviness 123

Chapter Thirteen
   The Formula for Depression .133

Chapter Fourteen
   "You Forgot Something, Elijah!" 141

Chapter Fifteen
   Protecting Myself from Depression 151

Chapter Sixteen
   Self-Inflicted Depression 159

Chapter Seventeen
   Letting Go of the Past 167

Chapter Eighteen
   The Depressing Giant of Unbelief 175

Chapter Nineteen
   Life Is a Choice 183

I'm Not Gonna Give Up on Me

"As for me, I will behold thy face in righteousness: I shall be satisfied, when I awake, with thy likeness." (Psalm 17:15)

A PERSON IS NEVER supposed to get to a point in his life when he says, "I've arrived!" Blessed is the man who has not arrived and knows it! Just because a person never arrives until he sees Jesus does not mean that he should sit still and say, "Since I can't get there, I might as well just let things happen." This type of attitude will only defeat and depress a Christian.

So many conflicts in life arise from conflict within. For instance, a husband and his wife have a conflict that causes strife and contention in the home; yet, 99 times out of 100 that strife is the outward reflection of an inward problem they have not reconciled with themselves. The Bible gives seven unique relationships a Christian is supposed to have in order to enjoy a complete and fulfilled life in his human relationships. The Bible describes these seven relationships in Ephesians chapters 5 and 6.

The Christian's first relationship is one with God. Ephesians 5:18 says, *"And be not drunk with wine, wherein is excess; but be filled with the Spirit.*" Every Christian must have a relationship with the Spirit of the living God. The Christian's next relationship is one with himself. Verse 19 says, "*Speaking to* **yourselves** *in psalms and hymns and spiritual songs, singing and making melody in your heart to the Lord.*"

Other relationships include the spouse relationship, the child/parent relationship, the employer/employee relationship, relationships between co-workers, and the relationships between brothers and sisters in Christ. God has ordained these unique relationships for every Christian to have a balanced life. All seven are vital; but the second one, a person's relationship with himself, is so very important. As a general rule, a person works on every relationship he has, but so often that second relationship is neglected.

A person's relationship with himself is so very important because a person is stuck with himself. An individual cannot divorce himself, cannot disown himself, cannot write himself out of his will, and cannot leave himself. A person can become schizophrenic, where he doesn't get along with himself, but the truth of the matter is that he would still be himself. No person can leave, abandon, divorce, disown, disenfranchise, or disinherit himself; he is one with himself. No matter how angry an individual becomes at the person in the mirror, when he walks away from the mirror, his self comes with him.

I know that I must live with me, and thankfully, a long time ago I realized that one of the most difficult relationships to cultivate properly is that of living with me. Truthfully, I just don't always like "me." It did not take me long to learn that when I do not like me, it is usually because I am having a hard time getting along with me. I also learned that when I have a difficult time getting along with me, neither do I get along well with others.

As a young teenage boy, I spent a lot of time walking in the woods with my hunting dog. At times I just sat on a hillside, and as I watched my dog run through the woods and the fields, I would just think. In fact, many of the truths and principles I now believe about relationships were formed when I was a young teenager.

I remember visiting at a friend's house and watching my friend disagree with his mom and dad. As I sat alone on the hillside, I wondered, "Why don't they get along? I get along with my friend, and I get along with his mom and dad. Why can't he get along with his mom and dad?" When I went to school and watched a teacher lose control of the classroom, I questioned, "Why is this happening? I can get along with that teacher, and I get along with my classmates. What is the problem in this classroom?" I contemplated for many hours about relationship difficulties, and I came to the conclusion that so many people have great difficulty in getting along with themselves. This inability for a person to get along with himself leads to many problems in life that could be easily averted. Allow me to share nine important thoughts about getting along with yourself.

1. I will not be satisfied where I am now. I happen to like me! Many years ago I came to terms with "me," and I learned to like me.

When I started traveling as a preacher, I realized that I would be alone often, and nothing in the world is lonelier than a motel room. In fact, I can think of nothing enjoyable at all about being alone in a motel. Watching television sounds enjoyable, but a person cannot watch it for hours on end and be right with God. Working is no fun. You sit alone in that lonely motel room wishing you had another human being with whom to talk. Once again, I came to terms with the fact that I like me. Because I learned to like myself, I even enjoy being alone.

However, just because I came to terms with liking myself does not mean that I was or am satisfied with me, because I never will be satisfied with where I now am. I like what one person said: "I'm not what I want to be, I'm not what I probably could be, I'm not what I will be someday, but bless God, I'm not what I used to be!"

Many people are down on themselves who have forgotten to look back and realize that they have come a long way, nor do they realize or consider what they will be someday. As the songwriter wrote, "This robe of flesh I'll drop, and rise / To seize the everlasting prize; / and shout, while passing thro' the air, / Farewell, farewell, sweet hour of prayer."

Those who work with people must realize that fact also. I cannot stress how very important it is to realize that even if a child is not where he should be, is he where he used to be? If you can answer that question "No," thank God because the child has made some improvement! I contend that even a backslider can backslide without going all the way to where he used to be. Be sure to give people credit where credit is due, and especially give yourself some credit for not being where you used to be.

2. **I will give myself a fighting chance.** In fact, I intend to give myself as much of an opportunity as I give any person who crosses my path. I watch people who work patiently and lovingly with underprivileged children. These people sacrifice and prepare some food or buy them a hamburger or take them on an outing. Serving others is wonderful, but do you ever do the same for yourself?

Christians sometimes feel like they are supposed to be an unfeeling spiritual machine that never needs a reward or a pat on the back or a note that says, "I'm proud of you." I must admit that I work on me far more than I work on anyone else, and I still need to be encouraged. Sometimes I stand in front of a mirror and say, "Schaap, listen to me. You can walk in that pulpit even if you have never been a pastor because you have over 20 years of experience with working with thousands of people."

That "psyching up" is what athletes do before a game. The coach pumps up the baseball players with chanting over and over, "We're gonna win! We're gonna win!" Christian, do you ever do that for your spiritual life? Do you ever do that for your marriage? Husband, as you drive home, do you say, "I am going to be good and kind to my wife and family." You psyche yourself up for everything that follows beginning with, "Hello, Sweetheart!" Pull for yourself! Give yourself the same kind of fighting chance! Often we are so willing to give others a little slack; but we have none for ourselves. To be sure, some people do the opposite—they give themselves all the credit and offer no leeway to anyone else. Remind yourself that you are worth investing in.

3. If I'm wrong, I'll go back to where I was right. If a person was spiritually flawless, could perfect every step in advance, and had no bad days, he would arrive at the end of his life as a perfect, computerized machine. Of course, no one can be like that, and human beings are prone to wander and stumble. The proper reaction to stumbling is for the person to go right back to where he stumbled and start afresh.

Unfortunately, too many people say, "I stumbled; I might as well just throw in the towel. What kind of fool was I to think that I could do that?"

Christian, don't get down on yourself! You have to live with yourself. You must get back up and get going! When a Christian gets down on himself and doesn't get back up, the next step he takes is to get down on anyone who reminds him that he is down. I am greatly bothered by those who take a detour and waste so much time talking about how they can never get back to where they want to be.

A man of God stumbles and perhaps forfeits the right to pastor. Instead of considering other available places of service, he spends the rest of his life being down on anyone who he remotely thinks is keeping him from the pulpit. I say, "Get back in the will of God right where you left it and do what you can do now for God!"

Ask yourself, "Where did I detour from the will of God?" Does your prayer closet have cobwebs in it? The simple, uncomplicated solution is to brush down the cobwebs and start praying again! Did you stumble in your Bible reading? Simply pick up your Bible and begin reading where you quit!

Years ago my dad and I were shoveling sand together. Dad had probably ordered about a hundred yards of sand to be brought in one day. All we had to move that sand with was our two shovels. Dad would soon get into a rhythm, and honestly, he could shovel sand for 12 hours without stopping. On the other hand, I would shovel for a while and start panting. I would stop shoveling, take some deep gulps of air, and begin again. Soon I would be leaning on my shovel gasping. All the while my dad was just consistently moving that sand.

Finally he said, "Son, let me tell you about pitching sand. It's a lot like the Christian life. It's not complicated; it's just hard work. If you get in a rhythm, you will do all right. See, my whole pile has been moved. How's yours?" Dad taught me a powerful lesson about living the Christian life.

God is not angry when a Christian stumbles; rather, He loves His children—He desires to have fellowship with His children.

He will do all He can to help the Christian who has stumbled to once again be in fellowship with Him.

4. If you can't go back to where you went wrong, just take the shortest route to right. Suppose a person marries, then divorces, and in so doing, feels he has discarded what he believes to be the will of God. Then he remarries. The answer to being in the will of God is not to divorce the one to whom he is now married!

Sad to say, sometimes Christians make mistakes from which they cannot recover. Sometimes a series of mistakes or detours makes it impossible for a Christian to be in the perfect will of God. The answer is to get back to right as soon as possible. He will never be what he could have been or should have been, but neither does he have to continue in the direction he was going!

Don't just be depressed and say, "I will never make it. I did not grow up in a good Christian home environment. I've taken a detour from the will of God." Workers are always needed on church bus routes; teachers are always needed in Sunday school classes. New ministries need to be started and built. In the Chicago area alone, seven million people have yet to be won to Christ. Unsaved people do not really care about detours that a Christian has taken!

A former pastor called me for counsel, and in the course of our conversation, he brokenly confessed, "Brother Schaap, I had a thriving ministry, and I lost it all. I just can't live with myself. I desperately want my ministry back. What do I do?"

Of course I hurt with this good man. But the truth is, he can never return to the place where he took his detour. Rather, he must take the shortest route available to right. "Sir," I said, "I don't think the people in the Philippines, or those in Mexico, or those in Canada, or those in India or China care about what you did 20 years ago. I have yet to hear about any Nigerians asking about a person's past. Those lost people whom God dearly loves are dying and going to Hell while you are depressed because you cannot have your forfeited pulpit. Face it! It's gone; bury it! It's time to get a new pulpit. Build one and preach in every tavern in your area. I doubt anyone will ask for your credentials. Stand on a street corner and holler!"

I'm sure this good man seeking my counsel was somewhat overwhelmed by my answer. What was I saying to this broken-hearted Christian? If you cannot go back to where you went wrong, then take the shortest route possible back to right, get on that road to right, and keep on going, keep on serving Him.

5. If I'm afraid about the future, I will review the past. Let me explain. In the will of God, the present, the future, and the past always have to work together in harmony. Someone stumbles, has a past that brings with it some baggage, and then he worries and worries about that past with its baggage. Thank God that Calvary covers it all! The songwriters knew well how to express the blessings of Calvary: "What sins are you talkin' about?" "Gone, gone, gone, gone; yes, my sins are gone. Now my soul is free and in my heart's a song."

Psalm 32:2 says, *"Blessed is the man unto whom the* LORD *imputeth not iniquity...."* The only past God sees is the old rugged cross where the blood of His Son was shed to cover every person's sin. A saved person's past is gone!

However, another kind of past is available—a past with no baggage! That is my past—a past with no baggage. When I was five years old, my sister won me to Christ. She took me through her version of the Romans Road, and I bowed my head and trusted Christ as my Saviour in September 1963. I bolted out of that bathroom to my mother who was washing the dishes after supper. I can still see the turquoise apron. "Mommy, Mommy, Mommy," I exclaimed, "I just asked Jesus to save me." As she listened to me, tears welled in her eyes. Even at five years of age, I remember the joy of being saved. "O happy day that fixed my choice / On Thee, my Savior and my God!"

I remember getting baptized three years later in 1966 because I was scared of the water's being over my head. In May 1975 at 1:30 in the morning during my senior year of high school, I surrendered to preach. It was like God enfolded me in His arms and said, "I want you to be a preacher."

I yielded and went off to a Bible college in Minnesota, and through an amazing miracle, I transferred to Hyles-Anderson College. I was then asked to work for the college, to be on the faculty; then came the position of a junior administrator, then vice president, and now pastor of First Baptist Church. All of the steps in a person's past are very important.

Every step in the will of God brings some fear. The Christian's tendency is to pull away from that which he fears. Most of a Christian's rebellion (or sin) is a byproduct of his fear of the will of God. Fear causes some Christians to flee deeper and deeper into sin until they bury themselves in sin. When the Devil brings paralyzing fear into a Christian's life, he has succeeded.

Christian, may I remind you that the future is always frightening. Instead of succumbing to Satan's trap, walk forward in the will of God. When fear comes and you feel like you cannot take the next frightening step, stop, look back, and review the past. That method is the antidote for fear!

When the pulpit committee of First Baptist Church called and asked me to candidate to become the pastor, I said to myself, "Should I become the pastor of First Baptist Church? Who am I to do that?" Instead of allowing fear to rule my decision, I stopped, looked back, and began a journey anew. I said, "I was five years old when I sat on the edge of a bathtub and asked Jesus to come into my heart and save me. That was a great day! I remember the duplex where my family lived on 139 E. 39th Street, Holland, Michigan, where I got saved. I remember when my pastor, Nelson Hill, baptized me. I remember meeting with God at 1:30 in the morning on May 6, 1975, with tears streaming down my face. I could almost feel God enfolding me in His arms. I remember how I thought I was going to die being loved by God, and I remember surrendering to Him after struggling for nine months. I remember surrendering my heart, my soul, my mind, and my strength to serve the King of kings. I remember my pastor advising me to attend Bible college, and I followed his advice. I remember my new pastor counseling me to transfer to Hyles-Anderson College. I remember the first time I met the young lady who would become my wife. I remember being asked to work at the college, then teaching as a full-fledged faculty member, then serving as a junior administrator and as the vice president. I was in the will of God then, and I am still in the will of God!" As I reviewed my steps, I realized that I walked into the pastorate of First Baptist Church of Hammond, Indiana, by His ordained will! I am exactly where God wants me to be!

Christian, instead of reacting right out of the will of God, go back to review how He led you all the way! In the Old Testament, God consistently reminded the children of Israel to remember the Red Sea. God was saying to His people that when their backs were to the Egyptians and they had no place to retreat, and when their forward side was to the Red Sea and they had no place to flee, they had to obey Him and go forward. When they stepped out in faith, they went through the Red Sea on dry ground.

Why remember the Red Sea? Because the past inspires me and assures me that I am in the will of God, and He will be with me as I face the next step. I received a card with an apropos phrase printed on it: "Do not be afraid of tomorrow; God is already there." I love that because if am afraid about the future, I can take a journey and review the past.

6. I will find my satisfaction in doing right, not in worrying how right turns out. That is exactly what Psalm 17:15 is teaching! *"I shall be satisfied, when I awake, with thy likeness."* Until I awake in His likeness, I cannot be satisfied. How do I live satisfied? Quite simply, I do right!

The Christian who does right sees a little more clearly all the time. A Christian never looks so much like Jesus as when he obeys and does right. If you are not satisfied with what you are now, all you need to do is do right! Satisfaction comes in doing right. The good feeling of doing right far surpasses the pleasures of sin for a season.

7. What God started, He promises to finish. Philippians 1:6 says, *"Being confident of this very thing, that he which hath begun a good work in you will perform it until the day of Jesus Christ."* If God is not giving up on me, what gives me the right to give up on me?

I Thessalonians 5:24 says, *"Faithful is he that calleth you, who also will do it."*

Philippians 2:13 declares, *"For it is God which worketh in you both to will and to do of his good pleasure."* The God Who created everything is working inside of you! Don't talk yourself out of something God started. If you are down on yourself, frustrated, or depressed, realize that God is staying with you to the end! You can't stop now! That point brings me to the next thought.

8. The only way I spoil God's plan is when I quit. When

you stumble, get back up, put one foot in front of the other, and keep moving forward. When a professional football player feels himself stumble and start to fall, he digs in and continues to push forward with every ounce of forward momentum he has—to gain any additional yardage he can. When the next play is called, he does the same. He keeps moving forward. When a Christian throws in the towel and says, "Enough is enough," God can't steer that Christian's parked, harbor-bound ship.

You must not quit on yourself, and certainly you cannot quit on God. *"I have fought a good fight, I have finished my course, I have kept the faith: Henceforth there is laid up for me a crown of righteousness, which the Lord, the righteous judge, shall give me at that day...."* (II Timothy 4:7) My father-in-law, Dr. Jack Hyles, penned a poem with seven stanzas entitled "Don't Quit" after listening to people say their burdens were more than they could bear. The statements he heard in one week's time prompted him to hate the word "quit" more than he had ever hated it. His aversion for quitting caused him to instruct the students at Hyles-Anderson College to cut the word "quit" from every dictionary on campus!

9. When I feel too unsteady to know what to do, I put myself on cruise control. Some people run in circles or to counselor after counselor, depressed and asking the same questions over and over: "What do I do? Where do I go?" When you are fearful, nervous, or depressed, put yourself on cruise control. Don't analyze the situation or yourself.

In all honesty, when I learned exactly how ill Brother Hyles was, I wept for more than an hour. I knew that I was entering into a zone I never wanted to enter. I knew I had to get up every morning and breathe normally. My wife needed to have a husband; my kids needed to have a daddy, and this ministry needed and expected to have a leader. I went through two weeks of hoping, then knowing, then the funeral and the memorial service, then candidating, and then accepting the pastorate of First Baptist Church. During that whole series of incidents, I stayed on cruise control.

How does that apply to every Christian? Attend church every Sunday morning, Sunday night, and Wednesday night, and don't question whether or not you should. Read your Bible every day whether or not you get something out of your reading. Go through your prayer list every day whether or not you get anything out of that time. Set the cruise control and just do what you know is right to do. If you just keep doing what you know is right to do, you will be satisfied. Take the path that God has ordained and don't quit.

Do not be satisfied where you are now. Give yourself a fighting chance. When you are wrong, go back to where you got wrong and get right. If you went too far into wrong and you can't get back to where you went wrong, go to right taking the shortest way to get there. If you are afraid about the future, go back and review the past of how Jesus led you to where you are. Find your satisfaction in doing right. Remember that what God started, He promised to finish, and when you get unsure or unsteady, push the button for automatic pilot and continue on cruise control. Applying these thoughts to your life helps you to keep working on you. Doing so will keep you from sitting down and quitting.

I work on me more than on anyone else in my life because if I am not right with me, then it will be very difficult for me to help another have a proper relationship with God. If I am not right with me, I cannot be a good husband and help my wife, who is the weaker vessel. If I am not right with me or if I am too preoccupied with myself, I cannot help those who cross my path. The person who does not keep himself right will never help anyone because he will be totally preoccupied with the greatest form of selfishness—trying to justify why he is not where he should be. Let's work constantly on staying right with ourselves.

CHAPTER TWO

RIDING MY FAILURE TO SUCCESS

"And I appoint unto you a kingdom, as my Father hath appointed unto me; That ye may eat and drink at my table in my kingdom, and sit on thrones judging the twelve tribes of Israel." (Luke 22:29, 30)

"Verily, verily, I say unto you, Except a corn of wheat fall into the ground and die, it abideth alone: but if it die, it bringeth forth much fruit." (John 12:24)

ONE OF MY GOALS during the difficult time of grieving through which the First Baptist Church family transitioned after the death of my predecessor, Dr. Jack Hyles, was to help the people with their grieving. I tried to do that even when I preached before I was called to candidate. How an individual grieves is very personal, and every person has his own way of grieving the loss of someone he dearly loves. Also, how a person grieves is his business.

My wife, the youngest daughter of Dr. and Mrs. Jack Hyles, and I were discussing the process of grief, and I said, "I think that a person may need as many as 25 years or more to grieve Brother Hyles' departure. Some people will take a lifetime to grieve because Brother Hyles meant a whole life to them."

A college student who arrived in the fall of 2000 and heard Brother Hyles preach perhaps 60 times will not grieve like someone who stood with him, like the Rock of Gibraltar from 1959 when he came to pastor First Baptist Church after pastoring four successful churches in Texas. That college student will not grieve like the person who continued to stand with Brother Hyles during the split and then on through some difficult times in the 60s, such as when the church building burned. Those who served with Dr. Hyles through the big days and through 1989, when a storm and a spiritual holocaust struck with this church in the center of the storm, will obviously grieve differently from those who barely knew Brother Hyles.

I realize that my opportunity to pastor First Baptist Church of Hammond came to me through the doorway of Brother Hyles' departure. To put it in human terms, my "grand" opportunity was caused by his grievous departure. My wife said, "I really feel very awkward and torn. I feel such a tremendous grief that my dad is no longer behind the pulpit; at the same time, I feel such a tremendous joy that my husband is. Both those conflicting feelings tug within me. One moment I feel the tears well up and begin to run down my face. The next moment I feel so thrilled that I want to shout, "That's my husband!"

That same tug of war that my wife feels so strongly comes, to some degree, to all of us who knew Dr. Jack Hyles. At his funeral service I said, "The only person who could do this funeral properly is the man for whom we are grieving right now. He's not here to do that." That expresses exactly how helpless I felt.

In no way did I want Brother Hyles to leave, but his departure opened a doorway which was God's will for my life. I fight an incredibly awkward feeling in my heart of "Am I supposed to be happy?" I can answer that question: "No, I cannot be happy about losing Brother Hyles."

On the other hand, should I be sad? Should I be sad because I am now the pastor of the First Baptist Church of Hammond? If the answer is "No," how then do I rejoice? Should I cry? This up-and-down labyrinth of emotions through which I try to find my way probably depicts how most people feel from time to time.

Another good example of this conflict of feelings came shortly after I accepted the pastorate of First Baptist Church on March 6, 2001. I was discussing some plans with the staff men, and one of them enthusiastically commented, "I haven't been this happy in 20…well…." His demeanor became subdued, and he weakly added, "Uh… I'm happy." I understood this good man's dilemma. He became excited about an idea's being implemented that was something he had wanted to do for years. It just so happened that we finally had the wherewithal to implement his idea. He got excited, but he felt he had to check himself and pull back because he also felt he should not be that excited.

The truth is, losing and dying and failing are always doorways that lead to winning, living, and succeeding. We just do not like that process. I do not like the process that catapulted me to the position of pastor of First Baptist Church of Hammond, but I am thrilled that God found me faithful.

For months after the Home going of Brother Hyles, every time I saw a photo of him, I wept uncontrollably. My spirit was so low, and I knew I had to get my spirit on topside. As I wept one day, I said, "Why did You do this to me?" I started thinking of an old song from that corny Hee-Haw television show. "Where, oh where, are you tonight? Why did you leave me here all alone? I searched the world over and thought I found true love. You met another and 'plththth' you was gone." I had to do whatever it took to get my spirit back. At times I tried arguing with God and Brother Hyles, and I said, "Preacher, it isn't fair. Look what you did to me!" My very next thought was, "But I am having the time of my life!" Losing Brother Hyles to death was the doorway that led to my opportunity to succeed. When I die one day, I am thereby opening a doorway for another, probably younger man to walk through.

Every person dies and hopefully leaves an inheritance for his children, or hopefully he leaves a legacy of his heritage. Every person should leave something worth carrying on. The only way the one who follows can truly have the authority or the power to carry on that legacy is by succeeding someone who has exited. By Brother Hyles' exiting, I was forced into a position where I can help carry the torch.

For some, the crippling events of life, like the loss of a loved one or an academic failure or a serious accident, become the catalyst for a sinful escapade that pushes them off the main track and parks them on a side track, leaving them feeling paralyzed. These crippling events—all of which involve losing and failing and death—are doorways that should be used to gain entrance to greater success, to greater winning, and to greater victory. That choice is up to the one who faces a crippling event of life like the First Baptist Church family faced with the death of their beloved pastor.

Success is present in every failure. Opportunity is present in every death. Victory is present in every failure. Victory is riding on the failures and using them as transportation or as a vehicle to the goal; it is working its way from beneath the failures.

Two different thoughts exist about success and failure; one is biblical and one is not. One thought says, "I have made a mess of my life with a chronic, besetting sin. I have tried many times to forsake this habitual sin, and as many times as I have tired, I have failed. I am waiting for some cataclysmic event, like a bolt of lightning from Heaven, to change my personality so I can become the person I have always wanted to be." For some, that cataclysmic event happens to be with the shattering of glass and the crunching of steel, and the person is paralyzed and literally wakes up as a new man—but not the new person he desired to become.

Waiting for some cataclysmic event or some act of God or some life-changing event to change a person is not biblical. God sometimes uses an emotional experience to change a person's life or direction, but the truth of the matter is, that experience did not change the individual's life; rather, God just got the person's attention for a while. Every decision made at an altar obviously does not change a person's life; the decision merely indicates that the person has decided he wants to make a change.

All that happens at salvation is that a person's eternal destiny is changed. Salvation does not change a person's character or his personality or even his disposition. That newly saved person is still the same person in the flesh that he was before he asked Jesus to save him. He now has the tools he needs to help him become a better person, plus he has a new Home in glory! When a newly saved person is baptized, he is not changed into a new person; he has merely followed the first step of obedience.

Many a person hopes that sooner or later suffering through failures or hardships or trials will make him a better person. That is not a biblical teaching; rather, the biblical teaching is that underneath every failure or loss or death, success is running like an underlying current. Though that current cannot be seen as failures can be seen, God is working to bring forth the success to His glory and His will.

Walking Through the Valley of Depression and Grief

I liken this underlying current of success to the tides of the oceans. A tide cannot be seen; the effects of the tide are seen. Each wave crashes on shore, and then it recedes. As each subsequent wave follows, it comes a fraction closer on the shoreline than the previous wave. The tide is the morning and evening whistle of the working day to the one who needs high water to leave or enter his safe harbor. Tides are the rise and fall of waters on a definite time schedule. From its lowest point, the water rises gradually for about six hours until it reaches high tide. Then it begins to fall, continuing for about six hours until it reaches low tide. The cycle begins again. The tide is the undercurrent of success riding on the waves of failure.

The cycle of failing and succeeding may not follow a definite time schedule. Adoniram Judson worked with the people of Burma for six years before he had one convert. Other missionaries experience immediate success on the mission field. Was Adoniram Judson a failure during his first six years as a missionary because he had no converts? Of course not! He was riding the waves of failure to success! He was learning the Burmese language that would enable him to translate the Bible into Burmese! He was laying the groundwork for thousands of Burmese people to be saved.

As a person fails and succeeds, the tide sweeps in beneath his effort and suddenly, low tide—failure—has become high tide—success! The continuous crashing and ebbing of the waves brought in the tide. I have seen those crashing waves while walking on a beach and watching for the tide to come in. I gave up, but when I came back six hours later, the tide was in!

What happened? Success is unseen; it sweeps in gently, powerfully, and surely on the waves of failure. God is working in us, with us, and underneath us. Let me share ten helpful statements about success and failure.

1. Don't magnify failure above what it deserves. Don't magnify death or loss above what it deserves. Athletes understand this principle. A player fails and magnifies it so greatly that he pointlessly does something like jerk off his helmet and throw it at the referee or say something out of line. Of course, he deserves the penalty that is called, that of his expulsion from the game. Usually that behavior causes deep regret at some point in the game.

I remember playing softball with a person who did not like a call, so he chased the umpire with a baseball bat, cursing him the entire time. When I reminded him that we were Christians, he felt led to curse me! I left the game. This is an example of a person who magnifies failure more than it deserves. He, like many Christians, has failed to keep in mind that losses are doorways to greater opportunities.

2. The major upsets of life are the doorways of greatest opportunity. I believe the greater the upset, the greater the doorway to the greater opportunity. In 2001, the First Baptist Church family sustained a great upset when Brother Hyles unexpectedly went to Heaven. When he went to Heaven, I believe a doorway opened to greater opportunity. Brother Hyles wanted First Baptist Church to rise to the next level.

3. Failure is the effort spent on an attempt. Failure is the wave trying to bring in the tide, and one wave alone fails to bring in that tide. One little wave cannot possibly bring in the tide, but all the waves together can!

When I became pastor of First Baptist Church in March 2001, I knew I had some big shoes to fill. I knew I could not possibly fill Brother Hyles' shoes, but I did know that all of the members of First Baptist Church collectively could fill those shoes!

30 WALKING THROUGH THE VALLEY OF DEPRESSION AND GRIEF

Every little wave brings the tide infinitesimally closer.

4. Failure should never cause despair; it should reinspire. A wave crashes on the beach and then recedes. If God gave that wave a voice, do you think it would say, "I am never going to do that again! I didn't bring in the tide." No! I believe the wave would rejoice, knowing it brought the needed tide negotiably closer and prepared the way for the wave to follow!

Brother Hyles often said that it is not where you are; rather, it is how far you have come and in what direction you are pointed. The little wave that gently laps at the shore is just as important as the big wave that crashes on the waterfront. Both are pointed in the correct direction.

5. Failures expose the weaknesses that prevent one from reaching his goal. Therefore, failures are my teachers, my friends, my buddies, and my allies. Failure and loss and grief and hurt are the best friends a person has because they reveal the weaknesses that hinder him from succeeding.

In 1867 a Russian electrical engineer named Paul Jablochkov lit the boulevards of Paris with arc lights. However, these lights were impractical for use in homes and offices. Thomas Alva Edison wanted to invent a substitute for gas, the chief means of lighting in the 1870s. The story is told that while Mr. Edison was still trying to perfect the lightbulb, a friend visited his workshop, saw all the discarded bulbs, and asked, "How many times have you tried to perfect a lightbulb?"

"Over ten thousand," was Edison's reply.

"Have you succeeded? Do you have a workable lightbulb?"

"No," Mr. Edison replied, "but I now know over 10,000 ways not to build a lightbulb." Edison said, "Many of life's failures are people who did not realize how close they were to success when they gave up."

May I ask if you know over 10,000 ways not to succeed at reading your Bible? Do you know over 10,000 ways not to be a soul winner? Do you know ten thousand ways not to be responsible parents? If no effort is made, there can be no hope of success. He who never fails has never tried! The only hope a person has at succeeding is attempting and failing. The wave recedes, but the tide flows in beneath the failure. By the way, after many failures, Edison finally succeeded in perfecting a lightbulb that burned for one full day. On December 21, 1879, news of his invention of the incandescent light astounded the world. Thomas Edison rode the waves of failure; his success was unseen; it swept in gently, powerfully, and surely on the waves of his failure. The world was profoundly affected by Thomas Edison's refusal to let failure cause him to be a failure.

6. **Losing reminds us why we "play the game."** Losing occasionally when playing sports reminds the athlete of what is really important in the game. Life is a series of losses that must remind the loser of what is really important in life.

7. **Death is a reminder of what is so important about life.** A person's focus automatically changes when he walks by a casket of a loved one. Because Brother Hyles went to Heaven without any real warning, he never had the opportunity to say goodbye to his beloved church family. As a result, many felt a lack of closure and had a very difficult time accepting his death. As I watched people almost resent his Home going, I could not help but wonder what some people learned from his life.

Is that what Brother Hyles taught by his life when he said goodbye to his mother, the second dearest woman in the world to him? For many years, Coystal Mattie Hyles was the most important person in his life. When he said goodbye to her, he taught something more than saying, "I can't get over her death."

Is resentment what Brother Hyles later taught when he said goodbye to his buddy, Lester Roloff; to his dear beloved mentor, John R. Rice; and to his dear beloved friend, Bill Rice? The key to accepting his Home going was to remember all that he taught that was so important to growth in the Christian life—read and study the King James Bible and apply the teachings to your life.

All grieve the death of a loved one. Everyone hurts. Death is a reminder about what is really important in life. When Brother Hyles was on his death bed, he grabbed my hand, pulled me to his side, and said, "Carry it on! Carry it on! Carry it on!" I want to carry out his wishes.

We may need to weep while we "carry it on." We may need to grieve while we "carry it on." We may need to hurt while we "carry it on," but we **must** "carry it on."

8. **Failure can only instruct those who have a greater cause for living.** I have learned that my purpose in life is what protects me in my problems. If I stumble because of a besetting sin and I do something foolishly, that which gives me grace to survive is that I have a greater purpose than just not sinning. My purpose or goal in life protects me in my problems.

I have watched people get so annoyed with a loved one who stumbles and falls because of a besetting sin. Sad to say, the main reason why they are so upset is because their only purpose in life is not to have their testimony disgraced or their reputation damaged. That is surely not the purpose of the Christian life. God did not save any person to model for Him as a perfected saint; rather, He saved a person to illustrate the fact that failure is success turned inside out and that success is failure turned inside out. When Jesus lost His life on the cross, His sacrifice brought great victory. Sin is always terribly wrong, but if that is the only truth we learn about sin, we are missing the overall picture. If we shouldn't sin because it is bad, then why didn't God make us all perfect when He saved us?

The Bible has so many illustrations and instructions about success and failure. *"For a just man falleth seven times, and riseth up again...."* (Proverbs 24:16) The person who handles the continual crash and receding of the waves will eventually see the kingdom coming underneath the tide! We have stumbled and fallen and failed and lost, or so it seems, and subsequently, we have a kingdom.

9. Satan contends that failure is permanent. He would tell every Christian that all failure subtracts from his purpose. As I start my journey in my Christian life, I must have a purpose. If I have no purpose, then soon my only purpose is protection. I must protect my ego, my reputation, and my testimony. If someone or something causes me to stumble, my sole purpose in life is to protect my damaged reputation. Instead of living a life of service for God, I fret, get upset, and am depressed. God's purpose for my life is not to see how perfected I can become; achieving my goal in life is His purpose for me.

What is your goal? Teach the Bible to your Sunday school class? Build your bus route as large as possible? Keep as many souls as possible out of Hell? Your goal is not to work on you at all; the goal is to work on someone else. The goal is to find someone who is depressed and pull them along on the journey with you. The crashing and receding waves bring in the current of success.

10. As long as you continually turn to Jesus, you are not a failure. If every time a person falls he turns his eyes upon Jesus, he has just won the battle. *"Looking unto Jesus the author and finisher of our faith; who for the joy that was set before him endured the cross, despising the shame, and is set down at the right hand of the* *throne of God.*" (Hebrews 12:2) Look to Jesus Christ every time you fail, and you are a winner. Instead of counting how many times you fail, count how many times you look to Jesus.

The average person focuses far too much energy and expends himself in a far greater way than failure deserves. The average person looks too much at failure. He spends far too much time worrying about past mistakes and far too little time concerned about his direction. Whether a person's failure is a moral one, a physical one, a spiritual one, or an emotional one is not the issue. Keep in mind that with or in every failure, success is cradled underneath in His everlasting arms. Why not let Him carry you to success?

CHAPTER THREE

HOW DO I WALK
THROUGH THE VALLEY?

"The LORD is my shepherd; I shall not want. He maketh me to lie down in green pastures: he leadeth me beside the still waters. He restoreth my soul: he leadeth me in the paths of righteousness for his name's sake. Yea, though I walk through the valley of the shadow of death, I will fear no evil: for thou art with me; thy rod and thy staff they comfort me. Thou preparest a table before me in the presence of mine enemies: thou anointest my head with oil; my cup runneth over. Surely goodness and mercy shall follow me all the days of my life: and I will dwell in the house of the LORD for ever." (Psalm 23)

WHEN I ACCEPTED THE call to pastor First Baptist Church, I was immediately thrust into a new level of leadership. Some of my employers became my employees. Co-workers with whom I had served shoulder to shoulder doing administrative tasks became my employees. I enjoyed a close personal relationship with many of these great men of God. Suddenly, I was no longer "Brother Jack" to them. While in a meeting with some of the administrators, one of them eventually asked, "What are we supposed to call you?" Before I could answer, he said, "I can explain myself. 'Preacher' will always be reserved in my heart for Brother Hyles."

His question and subsequent explanation did not upset me; I agreed with him. I know that a new generation will grow up with me who did not know Brother Hyles as well, and I will become their preacher. I wanted those who reverently, sincerely, intimately, and affectionately called Brother Hyles "Preacher" to keep that nomenclature in place. "Just call me Brother Schaap." He was content with my answer.

As each person has struggled individually with grieving over the death of Brother Hyles, he has had to persevere through other fears and griefs at the same time. Fortunately (or unfortunately) life continues on while a person wishes it could stand still so he could properly absorb one grief at a time. Life just does not stop; people are forced to move on with the momentum of living life. Several months after the death of Brother Hyles, my dad buried his brother; seven days later, that same family buried a daughter. Within a matter of seven days, my aunt had to lose a husband and then say goodbye to a daughter. She said what we all would say: "I really don't know how I can face the next five minutes, let alone the next twenty-four hours." My aunt already had an understanding of the stages of grief.

Trying to rush the stages of grief is like a farmer trying to rush a harvest; obviously corn cannot be planted in August and harvested in September. Farmers throughout the Midwest begin preparing their fields for planting in April and May. Some of them even have their planting done by the first of May. If a farmer does not have his planting finished by mid-June, he will, more than likely, be in trouble because he will not be harvesting in October. The laws of harvest cannot be forced, and grief, like the harvesting process, cannot be forced either. Grief is the cultivating of a more mature life under the direct guidance of God.

Grief comes like the rolling of waves. It can be like a rip tide, where a swimmer is caught in two opposing currents. The suction of one current pulls the swimmer from the shore and from stable footing; and the other wave pushes the swimmer, causing him to roll uncontrollably. The bottom of the body of water is usually rough and irregular, so the swimmer is further hindered from gaining his equilibrium. As he gasps for air and desperately looks for safety, the next wave catches him, carrying him even further from the safety of the shore. If only the waves would stop! The rip tide of grief engulfs the anguished soul. Just as he breaks the surface gasping for air and relief, another wave of grief strikes. If only the waves of grief would stop for a moment, the grieving one could regain his equilibrium—if only for a brief respite. Regrettably though, life does go on; it must continue.

In 2001 when Dr. Hyles went to Heaven, a huge tidal-like wave crashed over the church family. Many dear people wanted life to calm down—if only for a moment so they could get their footing and heave a sigh of relief—only to receive another semi-tidal wave flooding over them, such as a medical dilemma or a wayward child or the death of another loved one.

David must have felt much the same way when he said, "*Yea, though I walk through the valley of the shadow of death, I will fear no evil.*" David faced the valley of shadows without fear because he knew that God was in close proximity. Many of the fears of life are a nothing more than a valley of shadows.

Quite simply, a shadow is caused when any kind of mass intercepts light rays. A shadow has no power to hurt anyone. Obviously, the shadow of a gun cannot shoot; however, the shadow is evidence of a real gun! The shadow of a knife cannot gash someone of its own volition; but the shadow is a warning of a very real knife! The shadow of death cannot take a person's life; however, the realness of death is present. A shadow is representative of something very real at hand.

Nonetheless, the shadow was an indication that something tangible was present. David wanted to pass through that valley of shadows, and he learned that the best way out of the valley was to go through the valley. Too many people want to quit and flee from the valley. I have no doubt that David did not like his valley; still, he marched resolutely through, knowing the shadows could be faced with God's help.

Perhaps the best illustration of a man who went through the greatest valley of shadows was the man Job. The entire book of Job illustrates the 13 stages of grieving through which the man Job passed. Whether a person is grieving the loss of a loved one, or facing a medical catastrophe, or mourning a wayward child—whatever the grief—the book of Job teaches the 13 steps through which one must journey.

1. **The divine approval of a painful plan.** The Bible says in Job chapter 1 that Satan appeared before God. When God asked Satan what he was doing there, Satan told Him he had been on earth, *"going to and fro."* Before Satan could criticize anyone or anything, God said, *"Hast thou considered my servant Job?"* Just like God called Job's name before the Devil, I believe many Christians have had their names called by God before the Devil as examples of those who live up to expectations.

One of the greatest votes of confidence a person in the grieving process can have is God's bringing his name before the Devil saying, "I have considered My servant, and I want you to consider My servant because he is living up to My expectations." The first stage in grieving is when God approves a divine plan to allow hurt into the life of one of His children. God has never used anyone greatly until He has allowed him to hurt deeply. When great hurt comes to one of God's children, God's plan is to use that individual greatly.

That plan brings no great comfort to anyone who is going through the grief process. No one says, "I'm so glad I'm hurting because God plans to use me." When in the midst of great grief, that thought is probably of no comfort whatsoever. Nobody is glad that God has a greater plan for him when it involves great grief.

A lady who is grieving greatly said to me, "If someone else quotes Romans 8:28 to me, I believe I might react in a very unkind way! I don't want anyone telling me that things work out for good; that's what **I'm** supposed to say when **I** see something good happening."

As I thought of that good lady's sorrow, I am amazed at how incredibly inappropriate Christians can be when people are grieving. Another lady shared how some well-meaning friends came to her as she was standing by the casket of her husband and said, "I know exactly how you feel."

She said, "Brother Schaap, the person who said that had a husband standing beside her. She will get in a car with him and drive home. She will go to sleep with him at her side. The next morning she will have breakfast with her husband, and my husband is lying in a casket. She has absolutely no idea of how I feel! I know I probably shouldn't have reacted so strongly, but I cannot believe how people—even dear friends—glibly say, 'I understand.' "

Still another lady said, "I'm sure people mean to be sincere; but some are so totally inappropriate. When a friend of mine and her husband were standing beside the casket of their nine-year-old child, heavily grieving the unthinkable loss of their child, a friend said, 'I know how you feel; our dog died last month. We're still having a hard time getting over it.' "

I have no doubt these good people thought their sincere words would bring comfort. The truth is their attempt at comforting someone who desperately needed comfort was pointless. When going into a grieving process or coming out of a grieving process, it can be encouraging to know that God has appointed you for some special opportunity. However, when you are in the middle of grief, it really doesn't matter that God wants to use you in a greater way.

It is also important to remember that nothing ever comes to us without God's permission. We are immortal until our work is finished, and we cannot be harmed unless God "signs the memo" of approval. When the trial comes, we must understand that God saw the memo, read the memo, approved the memo, and then signed the memo. We may feel abandoned by God, but He has personally approved the journey through which we must pass. When the recipient of grief can grasp and accept—however difficult—the divine approval of a painful plan, he journeys onward to his next step of grief.

2. Automatic response. When Job went through the grief of losing his children, his investments, nearly all of his employees, and his possessions, he had to go on "automatic pilot." Job's reflex action to his horrific news was to say, *"...the LORD gave, and the LORD hath taken away; blessed be the name of the LORD."* (Job 1:21)

The reason why Job acted in that wonderful Christian way was that Job feared God and eschewed (abstained from) evil. His whole life was characterized as a man who feared God. God allowed Satan to try Job much like the rounds of a boxing match. In round one, Job lost—all of his possessions. He staggered to his corner and responded appropriately. In round two, he lost again—his health. Once again Job set the automatic pilot button, but his wife failed to do likewise. She revealed the level of her spiritual life when she uttered some words that condemn her testimony for all eternity. "...*Dost thou still retain thine integrity? curse God, and die.*" (Job 2:9)

Job responded appropriately to his wife's embittered words. "*What? shall we receive good at the hand of God, and shall we not receive evil?*" (Job 2:10) Job did not sin with his mouth. He responded exactly as he had been becoming. God knew He could trust His servant for round three.

When the rip tide of disaster and devastation crashed over him, Job reacted in a habitual manner and praised God because he had been praising God all of his life! However, unlike Job, many Christians react in a less-than-stellar way because they respond in the way they have been living up to that point in their life. I can promise that the person who has not been right with God will not say, "*...the* LORD *gave, and the* LORD *hath taken away; blessed be the name of the* LORD." (Job 1:21) More than likely the person will be upset with everyone, including God.

On the other hand, when the life of the Christian who lives on higher ground is touched by a catastrophic event, he will not buckle and acquiesce to the hurt, but he will keep on responding like he has always been responding. The automatic pilot a grieving person sets is an automatic indication of his spiritual life. What a person has been becoming is often unintentionally revealed. The pressure exposed what the person has been becoming.

3. Numbness. Modern psychologists call this numbness "clinical depression." When a person's emotional psyche seemingly cannot feel any kind of emotion, he has reached the stage of numbness. Usually, he cannot cry or laugh; he actually feels nothing.

The comfort brought by Job's friends beautifully illustrated the stage of numbness. Job had three friends that came to comfort him. When Job's three friends saw his acute grief, they were so disconcerted that they did not speak one word for seven days. I have no doubt Job's friends desperately wanted to say something comforting, but they were speechless in the face of Job's great anguish.

When a catastrophic event comes to any of God's children, numbness blocks out the sensations of life. A beautiful day is the same as an overcast day. Another's difficulties bring no feeling of empathy. The singing of birds is merely silence.

The numb stage can bring with it the feeling of being backslidden or of not being right with God. Those feelings have nothing to do with journeying through this third stage. Numbness came to a man whom God called righteous—Job. Relief from the incapacitating numbness comes when a step is taken into the fourth stage of grief.

4. Searching. Job was like an normal human being; he wanted to know why. Job 3:11, 12, "**Why** died I not from the womb? **why** did I not give up the ghost when I came out of the belly? **Why** did the knees prevent me? or why the breasts that I should suck?" Job 3:20 continues, "**Wherefore** is light given to him that is in misery...." Job 3:23 adds, "**Why** is light given to a man whose way is hid, and whom God hath hedged in?"

"Why? Wherefore?" Job asked. Job pleaded for answers as he searched for answers and solid footing. Searching for comfort, searching for answers, and searching for relief from the pain are natural responses to grief. When the heartache, heartbreak, and grief come, it is natural to ask, "Why? Why did this happen to me? What did I do? Did I do something wrong? Is God judging me? Is God punishing me? Is God testing me?" If God did respond with an audible answer, most would not be happy with His reply. Diligently seeking for answers is a normal part of the journey through grief. With the searching comes the next stage for the grieving one to travel through.

5. **Anger.** In the stages of grief, anger is as natural a response as the divine permission stage. If a person hasn't yet felt anger, it is because he is probably trying to ignore his anger. He doesn't want to admit that he is angry. Feeling anger toward God is another natural step in the grieving process. Feeling frustration and anger at God for taking a loved one to Heaven is normal.

The anger is a natural, emotional response to God's approval of a devastating event. When a loved one travels the journey of grief and reaches the anger stage, be patient! Angry people lash out at loved ones and make imprudent statements they really do not mean. Just like seeds planted in the earth need time to germinate and grow, the grieving one needs time to journey through his grief. With the passage of the anger comes a stage of contriteness for the hurt caused during the fifth stage of the journey.

6. **Guilt.** As Job assessed his situation, he said, "I've sinned. I must have sinned because all this doesn't happen to someone who lives righteously."

In today's times we say, "I wonder if I should have had the surgery," or "I should have had the surgery," "I shouldn't have let the doctors pull the plug," or "I should have let the doctors pull the plug," "I should have been kinder to that person," "I should have…" The guilt stage is as natural as the previous five stages of grief through which a person has passed.

The responsibility for his personal adversity falls on his already weakened shoulders. He assigns himself blame, "I should have...." With the passage of time comes a step forward to the seventh stage of grief.

7. Self-neglect. The period of self-neglect is characterized by carelessness. The person doesn't care how he looks, how he acts, or if he goes to work. A very typical response from people who grieve is "Why should I get dressed? Why should I try to look nice? The reason to do anything is gone." While in the self-neglect stage, the grieving one basically disregards the world about him. From this stage, he continues a journey on a downward spiral and enters the eighth stage, an emotional valley that seemingly cannot be shared.

8. Self-pity. Job said, *"He hath put my brethren far from me, and mine acquaintance are verily estranged from me. My kinsfolk have failed, and my familiar friends have forgotten me."* (Job 19:13, 14) Perhaps someone dear was taken suddenly. People will come to the funeral home and offer their condolences. Expressions of love and remembrances are spoken. Many people will attend the funeral. For a while, flowers and fruit baskets are delivered, notes are sent, and meals are prepared. But when all is said and done, those who offered their love and support must return to their families and their cares and concerns. Life must continue. The grieving one feels like everyone has virtually disappeared. The feelings of aloneness and desolation plunge the grief-stricken person into a deeper valley. Their thoughts automatically turn inward to "me."

The self-pity stage is one of selfishness. *"I called my servant, and he gave me no answer; I intreated him with my mouth. My breath is strange to my wife, though I intreated for the children's sake of mine own body.* (Job 19:16, 17) No one seemed to want to be in Job's presence while he was so self-absorbed. The truth of the matter is, no one wants to be around any person in the throes of a pity party! Invitations to a pity party are ignored. Still, self-pity is as natural as the previous eight stages through which the hurting one has already passed. Self-pity also opens the door to the ninth stage of grieving.

9. Self-righteousness. *"So these three men ceased to answer Job, because he was righteous in his own eyes."* (Job 32:1) Job reached the place in his grief where he questioned the hand of God. He told God that He did not deserve all that had transpired in his life. He became self-righteous and said, "It's not fair." In my opinion, most people take an average of six months to arrive at the stage of self-righteousness after the grief begins. A this point in the journey, God can step in and reveal why the hurt and grief had to touch His loved one's life. The door has been opened to the next phase of the journey.

10. Humbling. In Job chapters 38-41, God speaks to Job out of a whirlwind. The Words of God humble Job. *"I know that thou canst do every thing, and that no thought can be withholden from thee....Wherefore I abhor myself, and repent in dust and ashes."* (Job 42:2, 6) Job saw the power and presence of God.

For seemingly no reason, the Bible begins to make sense once again. The sun begins to shine brighter. A sermon warms the heart. Frustrations seem to disappear. The realization of what a self-righteous, self-pitying, self-neglecting, guilt-ridden, angry, searching, numb "victim" you have been brings you to the place where you do as Job did and apologize. "God, I'm so sorry. When I turned to You and felt You had no answers, I turned away. I know now exactly how much I desperately needed You." God had been waiting patiently for you to come to the point where more than anything you wanted to listen to Him once again! The eleventh stage of grief follows closely in the footfall of humility.

11. A fresh awareness of God. *"I have heard of thee by the hearing of the ear: but now mine eye seeth thee."* (Job 42:5) Searching for answers about suffering and pain in books did not assuage the grief. The various authors could only share their pain and their grief. One's individual, intrinsic pain cannot be compared to another's. Each must find his own way through the misty flats of his personal valley. The reality awakens the traveler to the awareness of the fact that God also traverses the valley with His child. The grief can finally be put aside as a relationship is renewed with God. The soul experiences an inward revival.

The definition of revival is a fresh awareness of God; it is like being resurrected from the grave. The joy of salvation has returned, and the love of God has become very real once again. To be sure, times still creep in when the grief returns, but those times become fewer and further between. The desire comes anew to share God's goodness with others.

12. A renewed desire to help others. *"And the LORD turned the captivity of Job, when he prayed for his friends...."* (Job 42:10) Job prayed for this three friends. His journey through grief arrived to the stage of thinking about others. "Others, Lord, yes, others, let this my motto be," the poet penned.

> "Let 'self' be crucified and slain
> And buried deep: and all in vain
> May efforts be to rise again
> Unless to live for others."

The inward focus turns outward, and thoughts are turned toward a dwindling Sunday school class or a bus route, to soul winning, to life itself. Those who have watched their loved one stumble through the valley of shadows say, "Welcome back! You were missed!" The renewed desire to help others joins hands with the final stage of grief.

13. Increased productivity for God. *"...also the Lord gave Job twice as much as he had before."* (Job 42:10) God rewarded Job with twice as much as he lost. The windows of Heaven opened to God's man, and blessings fell on him. Serving Jesus once again becomes a joyful activity. Oh, yes, the sadness is still present; the pain still lingers. Self-righteousness, self-pity, and self-neglect are little, ebbing shadows. The walk through the valley of the shadow of death has not been in vain, for the realization has come that He has made the journey, too.

The journey through the 13 stages of grief is not pleasant; rather, it is depressing and lonely and must be made, so be patient with yourself and be patient with others. If another who is grieving seems to be advancing through the stages more quickly, don't feel like you are not right with God; be patient with yourself. Give yourself adequate time to go through the entire journey, however difficult, of grieving. Keep in mind that God is taking the journey with you.

CHAPTER FOUR

PERFECTING YOUR FEARS

"Herein is our love made perfect, that we may have boldness in the day of judgment: because as he is, so are we in this world. There is no fear in love; but perfect love casteth out fear: because fear hath torment. He that feareth is not made perfect in love. We love him, because he first loved us. If a man say, I love God, and hateth his brother, he is a liar: for he that loveth not his brother whom he hath seen, how can he love God whom he hath not seen? And this commandment have we from him, That he who loveth God love his brother also." (I John 4:17-21)

F EAR IS A PART of the natural progression of grief and depression. Fear is as natural a part of man's life as is breathing. Fear cannot be avoided. Man has no power over whether the presence of fear comes or goes; he must simply deal with his fear. Very few people learn how to deal with their fears, and how they handle their fears will make all the difference in the world. Handling fear improperly can bring failure. In fact, written on the tombstone of many a man should be the words: "Here lies a man who failed because of fear."

Fears take many forms. People fear losing a loved one or facing the surgeon's knife or accepting new tasks or having too much responsibility. A person's overwhelming fear could rob him of a new responsibility. Fear of rejection, fear of acceptance, and fear of not finding a life's mate are just a few of the fears that can paralyze a person. Fear is an integral part of every person's life.

Fear is described four ways in the Bible. The first kind of fear, **paralyzing fear**, is encountered in Luke 19 in the parable about some men who are given responsibility. Two of the three men capitalized on the investment given to them and, as a result, had something to offer the nobleman when he returned. One man, out of fear, did not come through for his employer; instead, he offered excuses. *"And another came, saying, Lord, behold, here is thy pound, which I have kept laid up in a napkin: For I feared thee, because thou art an austere man: thou takest up that thou layedst not down, and reapest that thou didst not sow. And he saith unto him, Out of thine own mouth will I judge thee, thou wicked servant. Thou knewest that I was an austere man, taking up that I laid not down, and reaaping that I did not sow."* (Luke 19:20-22)

In this passage, the unprofitable servant is called wicked. Why would God get so angry at someone who is fearful? After all, the Bible says in Proverbs 1:7, *"The fear of the LORD is the beginning of knowledge...."* The problem was not the fact that the man feared his employer; the problem was the kind of fear—paralyzing fear. This man's fear was that he could not produce. Some fear is healthy; but paralyzing fear robs one of great opportunities. What would have happened if this man had succeeded? Failure is the wave which success rides to the shore. The issue is not about failing; the issue is not trying!

Luke 19:22-24 continues, *"And he saith unto him, Out of thine own mouth will I judge thee, thou wicked servant. Thou knewest that I was an austere man, taking up that I laid not down, and reaping that I did not sow: Wherefore then gavest not thou my money into the*

*bank, that at my coming I might have required mine own with usury?
And he said unto them that stood by, Take from him the pound, and
give it to him that hath ten pounds."* Today's society takes from the
rich and gives to the poor; in this parable, God said to take from
the lazy and give to the hard-working. Today's society tends to
reward the lazy man by taking the hard-working man's money
and forcing him to give it to programs that benefit the many who
refuse to earn money by the sweat of their brow. The average
man's tax bills are almost equivalent to four or five months of
salary. A large portion of those taxes are dispersed to people who
are basically too lazy to work.

Paralyzing fear is the emotion of a lazy man who does not
want to change or adjust his character to obey God. Though he
blames his laziness on circumstances or on the fact that his parents did not teach him how to work, his real problem is wickedness and laziness. *"The wicked flee when no man pursueth: but the
righteous are bold as a lion."* (Proverbs 28:1) The Bible says a person's refusal to take on a new opportunity is basically wickedness—laziness.

*"The slothful man saith, There is a lion without, I shall be slain
in the streets."* (Proverbs 22:13) Some say, "If I leave the safety of
my security, I might get slain." True! I believe it is far better to
die trying than to hide within the walls of security and never
meet the challenge.

On more than one occasion, my father-in-law discussed my
future with me. I knew what he hoped and dreamed and wanted
from me; however, I could only make one promise to him. I said,
"I do not know what the will of God is; but I can promise you
that I will not let fear make my decision." My promise not to
make a decision in fear satisfied him.

God does not want any of His children living a life of fear.

Paralyzing fear keeps many from doing His will for their lives. Paralyzing fear is nothing more than letting fear make your choices.

The second kind of fear is **panic fear**. *"Be sober, be vigilant; because your adversary the devil, as a roaring lion, walketh about, seeking whom he may devour."* (I Peter 5:8) The number-one weapon Satan uses against God's people is fear. He uses the instrument of fear to cause Christians to go into sin instead of being in the will of God. A friend of mine shared an illustration he heard a missionary tell about the roaring of a lion.

A missionary from Africa who was preaching told how the natives took him to the Serengeti, a vast grassland where thousands of species of animals range. Some animals of the Serengeti live out their lives feeding on the grasslands. Others, like lions and tigers, live out their lives feeding on the herbivores.

While they were watching some graceful gazelles, they heard the powerful roar of a lion. The missionary fearfully grabbed the native and said, "Let's leave." As he turned from the sound of the lion, the native stopped him. "No!" he exclaimed. "The motto in the jungle is 'run to the roar.'"

The missionary assured his guide that he wanted to go in any direction but toward the lion! The native wisely began to explain the meaning of the jungle motto. "The roaring of the lion unnerves the animals, and they begin to drift away from the roar. Soon they begin to flee from the roaring of the lion at top speed." The guide waited for about an hour and then stealthily took the missionary in the direction that the animals had stampeded. They spotted several lions eating several carcasses of the gazelles. The missionary was astounded because the roaring lion was in the opposite direction.

The guide explained that lions have two types of roars. One

kind of roar is a roar of triumph made by the young lions after they have killed their victims. The other roar is one to incite fear made by the old, toothless, clawless lions who are no longer able to take their prey. All they can do is scare their quarry into the quiet jaws of the young lions for the kill. How imperative it is to follow the motto in the jungle—run to the roar.

Our adversary, the Devil, was a roaring lion at Cavalry; at the tomb when Christ rose from the grave, the Devil was "de-fanged and declawed." The only way Satan can now hurt anyone is with fear.

Satan uses the stratagem of panic fear to scare a person into doing something very unwise. Panic fear is the emotion one feels when he is being tested. His fear of failure is so great he runs into sin and hides. D. L. Moody said, "Sin is basically man's attempt to hide from sin." To to keep from doing something unwise, he does something unwise. The downward spiral continues when he realizes he has done something imprudent, so he runs into something even more imprudent to keep from doing something more imprudent. Many who consistently run away from sin end up running right into sin. Fear creates an overwhelming desire to bolt and to run. Panic fears are based on past experiences that are immaterial in the present setting.

When I was a boy, we owned horses as well as boarded horses. My sister and I each owned a horse. Mine was a beautiful black, white, and brown paint named Chico. When we bought Chico, the owner failed to tell us that the horse had been hit by the milk truck. He also did not feel led to share that, as a result of the accident, Chico bolted and ran every time he saw a truck.

My dad owned property along busy Highway 40 in Michigan. The speed limit on that two-lane road was 45 mph; however, most people drove about 60 mph. We lived in a house on three acres of property, and we also owned a fourteen-acre pasture on the other side of the highway. Chico had been in the barn for the winter, and spring had come, so Dad said, "Why don't you take Chico down to the pasture? Put a halter on him, and use a long lead rope. Don't wrap that lead rope around your hands. If he happens to bolt because of the noise of the traffic, you can let go."

To get to the pasture, I had to walk Chico about a quarter of a mile along a two-to-three foot wide gravel shoulder of the road. Next to the shoulder was a four-foot deep ditch. My dad decided to follow Chico and me on a bicycle.

I went to the barn, put a halter on Chico, attached the 12-foot lead rope, and looped it in big loops around my hand. I grabbed Chico's halter and began to walk along the shoulder of the road, facing the traffic. Some cars were driving by, and I knew Chico was doing fine because his ears were pointed forward. As a rule, horses are generally inquisitive; and by watching their ears, their intentions are obvious most of the time. When a horse's ears are pointed forward, generally everything is fine. However, when a horse's ears begin to twitch back and forth, he is nervous about something. When a horse lays his ears straight back, that means get on, get off, or get out of the way.

As I was carefully leading Chico, I noticed a tow truck approaching in the distance. I knew by this time that for some reason trucks spooked my horse. As this tow truck rounded the corner about a half a mile away and began to accelerate, Chico's ears began to twitch back and forth. When I saw his ears alternating back and forth, I began to get scared.

Chico's nostrils widened, and he began blowing air in and out. I have no doubt that he smelled my terror. Just as that truck, which was traveling about 45 mph, was about 100 feet from us,

Chico decided to have a drag race with him. He jumped in front of me, spun around, and took off right in front of the truck. Chico jerked my hand off the halter, so I let go of the lead rope; however, he jerked so hard and pulled so fast, I didn't release the rope fast enough. The rope wrapped around my hand, spun me around, and I was pulled underneath the truck.

The driver hit the brakes, locked them, and the acrid smell of burning rubber was in the air. I could see the ground shaking and hear the screaming brakes, and I was terrified. The rope burned through my hands, and my horse won the race. I saw him standing beside the road, blowing air and shivering.

I grabbed the front bumper and pulled myself from underneath that truck. I stood up and looked right into the grill of the radiator. I walked to the passenger side, hopped up on the step of the truck, and banged on the window. The driver and the passengers were literally shaking like leaves. When the driver finally gained control, he said, "D-d-d-on't d-d-do that again."

Chico had a panicky fear that was based upon past experience. Since he was hit once by a truck, thereafter whenever he saw a truck, he automatically believed that truck would hit him. Chico was so frightened, and he wanted to avoid trucks so badly that he even jumped in front of them.

My sister, who was a born horsewoman, decided to cure Chico of his fear. I watched her make my horse do anything she wanted him to do—until he saw a cement truck coming. Chico decided to jump right into the path of that truck! He threw off my sister and literally crashed into the front of the truck, fell down, got up, and rammed into it again. Unbelievably, he didn't break any bones. My sister got back up on him, and he slammed into the truck again. Chico was so scared of trucks and so afraid of getting hit that he actually hit them to keep from getting hit!

Chico was not a stupid horse. As a matter of fact, when I think of Chico, I am reminded of people. A molested girl grows up, marries, and becomes very dominating in her home. She verbally batters her husband into submission in an effort to be sure he does not do to her what someone who should have respected and protected her did. In so doing, she destroys a marriage and a man while trying to keep from being destroyed.

A teenage boy is foolishly exposed to pornography, and as a result, that boy becomes an abusive husband and an adulterer. The fear of doing what he saw and didn't want to see caused him to do that which he feared.

The spouses in each of the cited cases are perplexed and confused and do not understand their spouse. Until you understand that my horse had been hit by a milk truck, you cannot understand why he is scared of all trucks. Being hit by a milk truck does not excuse Chico's behavior, but knowing his fear helped me as the owner of that horse to understand him.

The traumatic experiences one endures as a child or a teenager are sometimes locked deeply within the psyche of a person. No one knows about the situation except the one to whom it happened and the offending person. Others have some experiences about which several people know. They have sought counseling, attended seminars, and listened to preaching. Never once has it occurred to these people that the reason why they have that panic fear is that they are desperately trying to avoid and keep the hurt from ever happening again. A child of divorce grows up, marries, and becomes hyper-protective or jealous for no apparent reason except that the fear of divorce and the pain involved are so real.

Panic fear drives a person right into the very action he fears happening. It drives an individual directly into the waiting jaws of the quiet lions he feared. He ran from the roar hoping to escape, only to be devoured by the quiet devourer that was waiting in ambush. The Devil drives us by fear right into the very sin we are trying to avoid. As a result, we are devoured by the very fear of which we are afraid. The Bible gives an alternative in James 4:7, "...*Resist the devil, and he will flee from you.*" We can stand against the Devil, against our fears, against our imaginary dreams, and against the shadows lurking in our imagination from past experiences. Sad to say, most of our fears are self-fulfilling prophecies.

The third kind of fear is **productive fear.** "*By faith Noah, being warned of God of things not seen as yet, moved with fear, prepared an ark to the saving of his house....*" (Hebrews 11:7) Noah's productive fear motivated him to do as God commanded. Those who fear disappointing a loved one are motivated by that fear. I am afraid of bringing disgrace to my name or to my family.

Productive fear inspires us to learn. "*The fear of the LORD is the beginning of wisdom.*" (Proverbs 9:10a) Fear that inspires us to think, that drives us to do something productive, that gets us up early in the morning or keeps us up late at night, that makes us read our Bible and walk with God because we love Him, and makes us afraid of shaming His name is productive fear; it is good fear.

As I already mentioned, even though I am an adult, I still fear shaming my dad. I cannot imagine doing something so foolish that my dad would have to hear the news that I had to leave the ministry. That kind of fear is good; I also call it "running scared."

I personally believe that running scared is the best way to run as long as the person doing the running is not fleeing from the will of God. I am running scared, but I never want to bring shame and reproach to the cause of Christ. I want my family, my loved ones, and my friends to be proud of me.

The fourth type of fear is **perfected fear**. "*There is no fear in love; but perfect love casteth out fear: because fear hath torment. He that feareth is not made perfect in love.*" (I John 4:18) All fear has a certain bondage that incarcerates its victims. The Devil gleefully holds you in bondage as a prisoner when you allow panic fear to rule your life. You become a prisoner of your own fears when you have paralyzing fear. You are a prisoner of stunted growth even in productive fear if you do not mature beyond the fear stage. "*The fear of the LORD is the beginning...,*" but it is not the **conclusion**. A person starts with fear, but he doesn't have to end with fear. One who perfects his fear ends with love.

Having fear or a respect for authority is where one starts learning. Unfortunately too many people take a proud, disrespectful attitude toward authority, and a proud person cannot learn. I believe a person who struggles in a certain class would do better if he respected his teacher more. All learning starts with a healthy fear or respect but, in and of itself, that does not produce a mature person. What fear starts, love completes. How then can a person gain perfect or mature love?

I John 4:19 contains the answer: "*We love him, because he first loved us.*" The only man who did not run in panic fear at the crucifixion of Christ was the disciple whom Jesus loved. He did not flee because he knew the Man on that cross loved him. When a person gets so convinced that the people whom he respects love him, he will automatically stop operating with fear toward them; he will mature and grow. In the same way, when a person is convinced that God loves him, he will stand for Him and not be driven away by fear; he will mature and grow.

The burden is on leaders to convince their followers that

they love them. A leader with perfect love will convince his followers of that fact. A husband who has perfect love for his wife removes her fears. I John 4:18 says, *"...perfect love casteth out fear...."* One of the reasons why marriages suffer is that the husband or the wife is in panic fear based on past experiences. Perfect love could greatly help that situation. If the wife understood that her husband loved her, and she rested in his love; and the husband understood that his wife loved him, and he rested in her love, the panic fear would dissolve.

If Christians could ever gain an understanding that Jesus loves them, they would stop fleeing from His will, stop running into sin, and start being productive for His work. When a person becomes possessed of the truth that God loves him, his love begins to mature; as his love matures, his fears are replaced with confident love.

Too often our childhood fears define our adult love. Too often a wife loves her husband or vice versa out of the fear of what her parents did to her. Parents love their children out of fear of how they were treated by loved ones or on the playground. Because of those childhood fears, we lack a mature love that loves on the basis of the fact that He loves us rather than loving others on the basis of how we were treated in our youth. The great secret to overcoming our fears is to be baptized with the love of God.

God loves us! We are the objects of His love, His care, His devotion, and His affection. Parents, convince your kids that they are the objects of your love, care, devotion, and affection. Leaders, convince your followers you love them. Husband, convince your wife that she is the object of your love, care, devotion, and affection. Wife, convince yourself that your husband loves you. Wife, convince your husband that he is the object of your love, care, devotion, and affection. Husband, convince yourself that your wife loves you. Beg God to help you understand and believe that those whom you have been frightened of disappointing, scared of hurting, or scared of shaming their name, love you. Love will replace your fear and release you from the bondage of the past. Start saying, "He loves me, and because He loves me, I can do what He wants me to do!" The whole secret to the Christian life is hinged on how much you believe God loves you.

CHAPTER FIVE

WHY CAN'T I GET UP WHEN I FALL?

"For a just man falleth seven times, and riseth up again...."
(Proverbs 24:16)

IN PROVERBS 24:16, THE word *falleth* is thought to mean "to stumble" or "to make a mistake" or "to err." That is certainly not a totally wrong connotation, but the word in fact means "to slow down" or "to be overwhelmed" or "to be overburdened" or "to be unable to maintain the rhythm and pace being run."

At times the just man feels overwhelmed and heavily burdened. He sometimes feels like he must slow down in order to survive. But a just man will rise up again; he will find a way to get going again because getting back up is what a just man does. A just man seeks to maintain a balance in life.

The verse continues, *"...but the wicked shall fall into mischief."* The word *fall* in this portion of the verse means "to trip" or "to stumble." The just man does not trip or stumble; the wicked man is the one who trips and stumbles. For a legitimate reason, the just man is merely slowing down for a season.

Proverbs 24:17 adds, *"Rejoice not when thine enemy falleth, and let not thine heart be glad when he stumbleth....*" In this verse the Bible actually defines its own words in the verse; God is very careful to define the word *fall* by the word "stumble."

In Jude 24, "*Now unto him that is able to keep you from falling,...*" the word *falling* means "stumbling" or "tripping." The verse could be rendered "Now unto Christ Who is able to keep you from stumbling or tripping." God is surely able. The ability of God to keep us from stumbling is not in question. The Bible tells us line upon line and precept upon precept how a Christian can keep from falling.

1. You must build on your faith, not another's faith. "*But ye, beloved, building up yourselves on your most holy faith....*" (Jude 20) One of the reasons why a Christian trips and stumbles is that he has been riding the crest of another's faith. Riding another's faith is permissible for a young convert or a little child, one who does not have a lot of teaching and background about the Bible. Still, one who is new in the faith must begin to build on his own holy faith. If a person builds on the faith of another—a pastor, a hero, or a mentor—what happens when that person possibly passes off the scene? Quite possibly the person's faith will collapse. At some point in time, a young Christian must transfer his most holy faith.

When I was an adolescent child, God began to stir my heart. I did not wait until I was 40 years of age for God to teach me how to grow as a Christian. The only way a Christian can keep from falling is to build himself. He must build himself on his most holy faith. Secondhand faith does not build first-rate Christianity.

All of humanity is in a constant search for acceptance, identity, and security. I believe every problem in society is a byproduct of an individual's attempt to find acceptance, identity, or security—often from the wrong source. Gangs do not have the answer! Many athletes are plainly searching for a name, an identity, and security. However, the only way to fulfill these basic needs is to build on your most holy faith.

No one else can build your most holy faith; you must have a personal walk with God. Our identity is found in Jesus Christ. In II Timothy 1:8, the Apostle Paul wrote to 40-year-old Timothy, *"Be not thou therefore ashamed of the testimony of our Lord...."* Paul was saying, "Timothy, stop being ashamed of what I stand for." Faith is not being ashamed of Jesus Christ, His Book, His standards, His music, and those who represent Him.

How can a Christian keep from falling? How can a Christian get back up when he falls? He must build on his faith, not another's.

2.   He is to pray in the name of the Holy Ghost. Jude 20 concludes, *"...praying in the Holy Ghost."* As a rule, most people pray in Jesus' name. I believe that means that most pray to acquire their wants and their wishes and to change the comfort level in their lives. They pray to Jesus asking Him to modify the circumstances of their lives so that they might be able to enjoy it better, endure it easier, or have a happier life. The Bible says in James 4:3, *"Ye ask, and receive not, because ye ask amiss, that ye may consume it upon your lusts."* Our motives are often wrong, and we forget about the Holy Ghost.

The Holy Ghost lives inside every Christian; He knows every one of us intimately well. One way to keep from falling is to be completely honest with God—being completely transparent with Him. Too often we are too embarrassed to mention to God what is happening inside our heart and mind—as if He doesn't know what is in our mind.

Praying to the Holy Ghost means a person comes clean and honest with God in his prayer closet. He tells God about everything—the envy and jealousy and hatred and anger he feels, his conflicting thoughts, and the paradoxical emotions he battles. Being completely honest with God in the prayer closet will keep us from falling.

When you won't privately meet with God and confide in Him about your true feelings in your prayer closet, you will act them out publicly. You are walking through life trying to pretend that you do not have hurtful thoughts and ambivalent feelings. You pretend and pretend and pretend until you fall.

It is a wonderful day when a Christian comes clean with God and tells Him what He already knows! God is able to keep a Christian from falling; however, He is only able to keep him from falling if he will admit how close to falling he is feeling in his heart. Confession is just agreeing with God. *"If we confess our sins, he is faithful and just to forgive us our sins, and to cleanse us from all unrighteousness."* (I John 1:9) How sad when Christians won't privately confess their sins to God and have to face a public reprimand.

So many teenagers stumble and fall. They fail because they are acting out their Christian life. When they were 14, 15, or 16, they pretended and pretended and pretended, but they had no real faith. They were never completely honest with the Holy Ghost about their life. As a result of their pretense, they turn to what the world has to offer to belong.

It is imperative for a Christian to come clean with God. If he won't, he will be exposed to the whole world because God is not embarrassed to expose a person to his own sin. God orchestrated the scenario in II Samuel 12 when He placed David center stage to listen to Nathan tell the whole sordid story about David's adulterous affair. Since David would not deal with his sin, God exposed his sin for all eternity. God can organize the exposure of sin today as well as He did in Bible days.

If you confess to God privately, He will never tell anyone. If you will not tell God privately, He will expose it to everyone. *"But I say unto you, That every idle word that men shall speak, they shall give account thereof in the day of judgment."* (Matthew 12:36) Idle words are those which a Christian will not confess. God desires honesty from His children.

3. Don't require God to prove He loves you; require that of yourself. Jude 21 says, *"Keep yourselves in the love of God...."* Too many Christians regularly put God on trial to require Him to prove He still loves them. Calvary shouts His love through all eternity! He loves us once and for all.

Because human nature is so suspicious and so distrustful, every Christian must diligently guard the love of God so that he does not question His love. The Christian who manages to sever himself from the love of God can justify any transgression. "If God doesn't love me," he rationalizes, "who cares what I do?" He does love us, and that is why our behavior does matter. God says we are to stay in love with Him.

4. Be on the lookout for evidences of God's mercy. Jude 21 continues, *"...looking for the mercy of our Lord Jesus Christ unto eternal life."* What are some evidences of God's mercy? People's getting saved and baptized and living for Him verify His great mercy. People consistently walking to the altar and making decisions about their Christian walk are indicators of His mercy.

Christian, do you want to keep from falling? If you do fall, it will be because you were not looking for the goodness of God. People don't fall into sin who are looking for the goodness of God. The only place a Christian should fall is at an altar where he thanks God for how good He has been. When he starts looking and notices how good God is, he will stop looking at the deception the Devil has to offer. Being aware of what God is doing will keep a Christian from stumbling!

5. Be on the lookout for ways to show mercy towards others. Not only should we look at the evidence of God's mercy in our lives, but we should look for ways to show mercy to others. Those who spend their lives trying to help others seem to stay out of sin.

Look for someone who has a need, and be the one who fills that need. If you looked for people who needed someone to show them mercy, you would soon find that you would not need God's mercy for yourself. You will find in the lives of others all the evidences of His great mercy that you need to keep from falling.

6. Live for others, regardless of how you feel about them. *"And of some have compassion, making a difference: And others save with fear, pulling them out of the fire; hating even the garment spotted by the flesh."* (Jude 22, 23) In doing a word study on this verse, I discovered that the words mean that even if you feel discrimination in your heart toward other people, help them anyway. God makes no distinctions; He says to have compassion on all.

Not having a burden for people is not an acceptable reason for not helping others. Do not wait until God gives you a burden to start helping people. If you wait until you get a so-called burden to help others, you will never help another. You will never get a burden because you only get a burden when you start helping others. The Bible teaches to live for others regardless of how you feel about them.

7. Let the failures of others provoke you to humility and gratitude, not to envy and arrogance. *"Rejoice not when thine enemy falleth, and let not thine heart be glad when he stumbleth: Lest the LORD see it, and it displease him, and he turn away his wrath from him."* (Proverbs 24:17, 18) If you want to keep from falling, then do not be happy about another's misfortune.

For instance, it brings me no joy to think of anyone receiving judgment at the hand of God. I personally believe that AIDS is a judgment by the hand of God, and I am deeply saddened that God has had to go to such great lengths to judge people for being so wicked. However, every homosexual is someone's son, someone's brother, someone's relative, or someone's friend. To be sure, that lifestyle brings shame and disgrace to a family, but that person is loved by someone. Sodomy is a sin like adultery or fornication or cursing or laziness are sins. God hates the sin of sodomy, and AIDS is a judgment of God on a sin that He hates, but God loves sinners. *"But God commendeth his love toward us, in that, while we were yet sinners, Christ died for us."* (Romans 5:8) We are just sinners saved by grace. Arrogance has no place in the Christian's life.

If you want to keep from falling, you had better keep a humble, grateful spirit. Humility says, "Friend, may I help you? God loves you, and I do, too." Every time you see someone fall—enemy or friend—have some humility and show some gratitude that you are not in the same place. Only God's grace prevents us from falling. Christians surely need to show a whole lot more gratitude in their Christianity, rather than arrogance and pride.

I am not one iota happy when another is afflicted or hurt; rather, I am very saddened for that person. Neither am I happy when backsliders and rebels are punished and chastened by God; I grieve and hurt for them. *"Then came the word of the LORD unto Samuel, saying, It repenteth me that I have set up Saul to be king: for he is turned back from following me, and hath not performed my commandments. And it grieved Samuel; and he cried unto the LORD all night."* (I Samuel 15:10, 11) The Bible says Samuel grieved greatly for Saul even after God removed His blessing from Saul's life.

Samuel continued to pray for Saul to the point where God questioned him. *"And the LORD said unto Samuel, How long wilt thou mourn for Saul, seeing I have rejected him from reigning over Israel?..."* (I Samuel 16:1) Just like Samuel grieved for King Saul in his failures, we are to allow the failures of others to provoke us to humility and gratitude—not to envy and arrogance.

The book of Jude teaches that God is able to keep anyone from falling, but we have to qualify for His assistance.

CHAPTER SIX

WHERE WAS GOD IN THE DAY OF MY TROUBLE?

"I cried unto God with my voice, even unto God with my voice; and he gave ear unto me. In the day of my trouble I sought the LORD: my sore ran in the night, and ceased not: my soul refused to be comforted. I remembered God, and was troubled: I complained, and my spirit was overwhelmed. Selah. Thou holdest mine eyes waking: I am so troubled that I cannot speak. I have considered the days of old, the years of ancient times. I call to remembrance my song in the night: I commune with mine own heart: and my spirit made diligent search. Will the LORD cast off for ever? and will he be favourable no more? Is his mercy clean gone for ever? doth his promise fail for evermore? Hath God forgotten to be gracious? hath he in anger shut up his tender mercies? Selah. And I said, This in my infirmity: but I will remember the years of the right hand of the most High. I will remember the works of the LORD: surely I will remember thy wonders of old. I will meditate also of all thy work, and talk of thy doings. Thy way, O God, is in the sanctuary: who is so great a God as our God? Thou art the God that doest wonders: thou hast declared thy strength among the people. Thou hast with thine arm redeemed thy people, the sons of Jacob and Joseph. Selah. The waters saw thee, O God, the waters saw thee; they were afraid: the depths also were troubled. The clouds

poured out water: the skies sent out a sound: thine arrows also went
abroad. The voice of thy thunder was in the heaven: the lightnings
lightened the world: the earth trembled and shook. Thy way is in the
sea, and thy path in the great waters, and thy footsteps are not known.
Thou leddest thy people like a flock by the hand of Moses and Aaron."
(Psalm 77)

PSALM 77, WHICH WAS written by David, is probably
one of the most revealing looks at the humanness of a man of
God. Other Psalms show the heart and mind of David, but none
reveal his vulnerability, frustration, and depression like Psalm 77.
This chapter could also be titled, "What to Do When God
Forgets to Play His Role."

When my father-in-law pastored First Baptist Church, he
often mentioned how he was inundated with mail. I now understand his situation completely because every week my office is
deluged with letters and notes and cards. The messages in the
mail vary, but not a day goes by that I do not receive a letter saying something like, "The tests came back with bad news." Like
David, many of these people who write are in a stage of wondering, "Did God forget about me? Did He go go AWOL?"
Something assuredly happened to David that drove him to seek
God, but he felt as if God had failed him. David could not understand God's silence because he knew he needed the presence of
God to help him make some difficult decisions.

David was called "the man after God's own heart." He was a
man of God known for believing and trusting in God; he had a
record for God's coming through and using him, but God didn't
come through for him in Psalm 77. What do you do when all of
your hope is on God, and He seemingly is not hearing your cry?

David explains in Psalm 77 what to do if the day comes when God forgets to play His role—the day when God fails you in that day of your trouble.

The questions will plague your mind. Has God become bored with playing God? Has He become disinterested in His role in our lives? Has He grown old and tired and worn out and is now unable to perform His tasks? Sometimes we want to take God's face in both of our hands and say, "God, please help me. You are helping everyone else! How about helping me?"

Perhaps you think the problem is that He is angry and has given up trying to help you. Maybe He has said, "Forget it; I've helped you over and over, and you never learn. I'm never going to help you again."

If you never have felt these types of feelings, then your day of trouble has never come to you. If you say of what I have described, "That is exactly how I feel," you are describing a day of trouble that has come into your life. Every one of us has a description of how we believe God should behave in any given circumstance, and when God does not come through as we anticipated He would, we are literally stunned that He did not play His role properly. We look toward Heaven and say, "God, where are You?"

According to Psalm 77, David obviously had a day of trouble where he felt he could not find God. He could not find comfort for his soul, he could not rid himself of his depression, and he could not sleep at night. No other human being could bring comfort to him either. What happens when you try to find the right answers and they do not work? You then go to Jesus, but what if Jesus does not come through for you?

If you have not come to the point in your Christian life when you have almost shaken your fist and said, "God, You might kill me for saying this, but You are not coming through," you have not yet had a day of trouble. If you have not found yourself griping and complaining and even scolding God, you have not yet had a day of trouble.

David said he hurt so badly that he could not even speak. Have you ever hurt that badly? Have you ever hurt so much that all you can do is enter your prayer closet and groan? David tried the balm of music. Perhaps a certain song had previously rejuvenated him. This time in his day of trouble, even music failed him. David tried other ways to renew his spirit—to no avail. He tried to convince himself that he was getting better, but in his heart he knew he was only getting worse. Perhaps he tried some "new" avenue of help and attended some self-help seminars or read some self-help books.

I love what Dr. J. Vernon McGee, a famous radio preacher from years ago, told about a tough time he was having in his life. He went to a self-help seminar, and the motivational speaker told the attendees to go home, go to bed, get up the next morning, go in the bathroom, turn on the lights, shut the door, look in the mirror, and say, "I love you! You're the best thing that ever happened to me! You are my friend. You and I are going to make it! We're getting better and better every day."

Dr. McGee decided to try what the speaker advised. So he went home, went to bed, got up in the morning, walked in the bathroom, turned on the lights, shut the door, looked in the mirror, and said, "You! You! I don't love you! I don't even like you! You're my worst enemy; you've let me down again and again and again! The only thing good about you is Jesus!" When Dr. McGee left the bathroom, he said, "That self-help seminar didn't help me at all."

What did David do? He had griped to God, complained to

others, insulted the friends who tried to help, and still had no answers. What exactly did David do in his time of trouble? How does a Christian deal with his time of trouble?

1. Decide to face your problem and embrace it. *"And I said, This is my infirmity...."* (Psalm 77:10) The word *infirmity* means "rub." Even though the solution to his untenable situation surely rubbed him the wrong way, David decided to accept that which he did not want nor desire.

The word *infirmity* also means "sickness" or "weakness" or "that which wears me down." David's grief and pain wore him down to the point that he did not want any part of it. He tried to get rid of it and to push it far away from him, but it kept returning. David came to the realization that he could not conquer the difficulty, so he made peace with his problem. "This is my infirmity," he conceded to God. He realized that the problem was his, no one else's—not even God's problem.

The Apostle Paul endured and embraced the same kind of infirmity. II Corinthians 12:7-9 says, *"And lest I should be exalted above measure through the abundance of the revelations, there was given to me a thorn in the flesh, the messenger of Satan to buffet me, lest I should be exalted above measure. For this thing I besought the Lord thrice, that it might depart from me. And he said unto me, My grace is sufficient for thee...."*

Three times Paul prayed for God to take away what he called a thorn in his flesh, but God did not; so Paul finally accepted the fact that God wanted him to have the struggle of an infirmity. He learned to accept and live with his problem.

2. Remember the times when God did come through for you. Perhaps God did not come through this particular time addressed in Psalm 77 and answer David's prayers, but there were definitely many times when God did come through for His beloved servant. In the day of trouble, remember all the times when God did hear and answer your prayers. Be careful in the day of trouble, or you might forget all of the good things that God has done for you.

David remembered when he was a teenage boy working as a shepherd for his father. He remembered the time the marauding bear and the roaring lion came to ravage his father's herds. David conquered both of the animals in the power of the Lord. David also remembered the battle with Goliath and the surge of energy—the power of God—that came upon him when he met the arrogant Philistine on the field of battle. *"Then said David to the Philistine, Thou comest to me with a sword, and with a spear, and with a shield: but I come to thee in the name of the LORD of hosts, the God of the armies of Israel, whom thou hast defied. This day will the LORD deliver thee into mine hand; and I will smite thee, and take thine head from thee; and I will give the carcases of the host of the Philistines this day unto the fowls of the air, and to the wild beasts of the earth; that all the earth may know that there is a God in Israel."* (I Samuel 17:45, 46) The battle was the Lord's! *"So David prevailed over the Philistine with a sling and with a stone, and smote the Philistine, and slew him; but there was no sword in the hand of David. Therefore David ran, and stood upon the Philistine, and took his sword, and drew it out of the sheath thereof, and slew him, and cut off his head therewith. And when the Philistines saw their champion was dead, they fled."* (I Samuel 17:50, 51) David recalled all the times God had prevailed on his behalf. In the same way that God came through for David, He has come through for you—scores of times!

3. Remember all the times when God came through for others. Mrs. Marlene Evans, the first dean of women at Hyles-Anderson College, received her first of five diagnoses of cancer in 1982. To the amazement of her doctors, she battled the killer cancers for over 20 years! God came through for Marlene Evans, and He can come through for you. After all, God is in the miracle-working business!

God has repaired failing marriages. God has brought wayward children home. God has healed when there was no hope of healing. Even if it seems that God doesn't want to come through for you, you can rejoice and admit that He does come through for others. What God has done for others cannot be overlooked or disregarded as we stay steady in our Christian walk.

4.   **Remember the times addressed in the Bible when God came through for the Bible people.** Naaman, the captain of the army, was covered from head to toe with leprosy. Knowing how much her master hated his offensive condition, his Hebrew maid advised him to go and seek the help of Elisha the prophet. Rather than answer Naaman himself, Elisha sent his servant Gehazi with a message for Naaman to dip seven times in the Jordan River. When Naaman resisted the servant's words, his Hebrew servant again urged him to do as Elisha had ordered. Because Naaman obeyed, he was healed from his leprosy.

A man with a lunatic son brought him to the disciples and explained his son's suicidal nature. When he begged them to heal his son, the disciples could not get their prayers answered. In desperation the man went to Jesus for help. Jesus asked the father if he believed that He (Jesus) could heal the lunatic son. The man answered Jesus truthfully. *"...Lord, I believe; help thou mine unbelief."* (Mark 9:24) The father's little bit of faith moved Jesus to cure the stricken boy.

Many times in the Bible the people did not possess a great faith. When Peter had been arrested by the Roman government for preaching and was locked in jail in stocks, handcuffed between two soldiers, and in the inner sanctuary of the cell, the church people banded together to pray for his release. God heard the prayers of the people and sent an angel to free Peter. His chains fell off, the stocks disengaged, the door magically opened, he walked outside, and the gate opened. Peter walked out a free man, and he went to the church. When he knocked on the door, a teenage girl answered, saw Peter, hurried back to where the people were praying, and excitedly announced that Peter was at the front gate. The people did not believe her and continued petitioning God for the release of Peter. These people had a great amount of unbelief, but their little bit of faith moved God to release Peter from jail!

When I think how God has come through for me at times, how He has come through for many other people, and how He came through for the people in Bible times, I am reassured that He will come through—maybe not in my time frame—during my day of trouble.

5. I will tell others what I remembered. Maybe God is seemingly not coming through in a day of trouble, but we can share about the times He has come through. Start telling other people your memories of how God did come through for others.

6. I will expect God to give me answers through the pastor and his preaching. David said, "*Thy way, O God, is in the sanctuary....*" (Psalm 77:13) In Bible days, the sanctuary was the house of God. In this day, the house of God is the local church. David knew he could find answers in the church house, listening to the man of God.

When times of trouble come and you don't know where to turn, stay in the rhythm of attending church on Sunday morning, Sunday night, and Wednesday night. Eventually during one of those services, an answer will come from the pulpit, and you will say, "This is exactly what I needed to hear." Church is like a spiritual hospital where one receives spiritual medicine to survive a little longer.

Complain to God. Tell God your argument. Pour out all your depressing emotions to Him. Tell Him everything you feel because God is a big enough God to handle your diatribe. Unlike human beings, God doesn't get His feelings hurt and sulk. God knows what we are facing, and He is tough enough to handle our heartaches. He can take the complaining; just don't quit on Him. Keep on keeping on! Our job is not to tell God how we anticipated His coming through; our job is to eventually learn and grow and mature and begin to understand.

God has never gone AWOL in anyone's life. He seemingly may not be coming through like you anticipated He would, but He does come through, and He will make a way for you.

"Got any rivers you think are uncrossable?

Got any mountains you can't tunnel thru?

God specializes in things tho't impossible;

He does the things others cannot do."

God will take care of you—maybe not necessarily in the way you tell Him to care for you, but you will understand—in His time.

CHAPTER SEVEN

FEELING AT HOME
IN THE SHADOWS

"He that dwelleth in the secret place of the most High shall abide under the shadow of the Almighty. I will say of the Lord, He is my refuge and my fortress: my God; in him will I trust. Surely he shall deliver thee from the snare of the fowler, and from the noisome pestilence. He shall cover thee with his feathers, and under his wings shalt thou trust: his truth shall be thy shield and buckler. Thou shalt not be afraid for the terror by night; nor for the arrow that flieth by day; Nor for the pestilence that walketh in darkness; nor for the destruction that wasteth at noonday. A thousand shall fall at thy side, and ten thousand at thy right hand; but it shall not come nigh thee. Only with thine eyes shalt thou behold and see the reward of the wicked. Because thou hast made the Lord, which is my refuge, even the most High, thy habitation; There shall no evil befall thee, neither shall any plague come nigh thy dwelling. For he shall give his angels charge over thee, to keep thee in all thy ways. They shall bear thee up in their hands, lest thou dash thy foot against a stone. Thou shalt tread upon the lion and adder: the young lion and the dragon shalt thou trample under feet. Because he hath set his love upon me, therefore will I deliver him: I will set him on high, because he hath known my name. He shall call upon me, and I will answer him: I will be with him in trouble; I will *deliver him, and honour him. With long life will I satisfy him, and shew him my salvation."* (Psalm 91)

THE 91ST PSALM (OR SONG) was written by Moses, the man who led the children of Israel out of Egypt, across the Red Sea, through a miraculous parting of the waters, to the Promised Land. Moses led a population of 3½ million people, a number equivalent to the size of the city of Chicago, on a journey roughly the distance from Chicago to Detroit—through Lake Michigan! His leadership was amazing.

This journey could have taken the children of Israel about three weeks, but because of all the logistics and because of some training God intended for them to receive, the journey would take at the most 16 months. However, because of their rebellion and their unwillingness to learn what God had given them, the journey took them 40 years. God brought them out of Egypt, and Moses was commanded to take them to an area that absolutely was inhospitable. Even the nomadic tribes deliberately avoided that desert region of extreme temperatures where the daytime peaks at 135 degrees and then plummets to 35 or 40 degrees in the evening.

The logistics of this journey of 3½ million people are inconceivable. On an average day more than 200 died and more than 200 were born in the wilderness. Just the problems with the hygiene and medical facilities are staggering, let alone caring for the millions of animals needed for offerings, sacrifices, and food.

To help His people cope with the extreme temperatures, during the day God provided a massive column of cloud that cast a shadow over the majority of the children of Israel. God commanded Moses to stay in the middle of that shadow and to lead them from that vantage point. About 6:00 in the evening, that huge column of cloud ignited into a huge burning pillar of fire that gently warmed the people much like a giant warming oven.

The visual imagery of Moses' words, *"He that dwelleth in the secret place of the most High shall abide under the shadow of the Almighty,"* is so significant. Moses was saying, "I am under God's shadow; it protects me from the heat of the sun; it takes the chill from the evening air and warms me."

To abide under a shadow implies that something or someone has come between you and the source of light. In Psalm 91:1, Moses is saying that it is good to stand in the shadow. I personally believe that most people would rather stand in full sunlight than in the shadows. Though most of us love the sunshine and would not naturally choose the shadows, certainly some have been called to the shadows—to live in the shadow of someone or to live in the shadow of something that stands between God and them. Sometimes God chooses to place someone in the shadows. I believe that living in another's shadow is an awkward position in which to live. However, that is the calling of many Christians.

However awkward living in the shadows may seem, there are some benefits to living under a shadow.

1. **There is great security living in a shadow.** *"Thou shalt not be afraid for the terror by night; nor for the arrow that flieth by day."* (Psalm 91:5)

2. **There is protection under the shadow.** *"He shall cover thee with his feathers, and under his wings shalt thou trust: his truth shall be thy shield and buckler."* (Psalm 91:4)

3. **There is great safety under the shadow.** *"A thousand shall fall at thy side, and ten thousand at thy right hand; but it shall not come nigh thee."* (Psalm 91:7) In this verse, Moses was remembering some of the plagues sent by God to punish His disobedi-

ent people. In just one day 23,000 people died. Another time when thousands of other people were dying, Moses told the people to stand in the shadow; those who chose to live under the shadow would be safe.

4. There is great deliverance living under the shadow. *"Surely he shall deliver thee from the snare of the fowler, and from the noisome pestilence."* (Psalm 91:3) The *"noisome pestilence"* is a raging epidemic. Those who live under the shadow will be delivered from the plague.

5. There is tremendous insight and perception given. *"He that dwelleth in the secret place...."* (Psalm 91:1) The person living in the shadows learns the secret things of God.

6. There is tremendous victory. *"Thou shalt tread upon the lion and adder: the young lion and the dragon shalt thou trample under feet."* (Psalm 91:13) If the Devil comes as a roaring lion, stay in the shadow for the victory God brings.

7. There is promotion in the shadow. *"He shall call upon me, and I will answer him: I will be with him in trouble; I will deliver him, and honour him."* (Psalm 91:15) Honor is found when one is willing to abide in the shadow.

How does one abide under the shadow of the Almighty? *"He that dwelleth in the secret place of the most High shall abide under the shadow of the Almighty."* (Psalm 91:1) Allow me to paraphrase this beautifully written verse: "He that marries (or settles in) the secret place shall find a home and lodging in the shadow of God." The words *secret place* and the word *shadow* have almost the same meaning. God was saying that if you make the shadow your home, you will live there with security, protection, safety, deliverance, victory, perception, and promotion!

The word *abide* has a double meaning. It means "to find home," and it also means "to make bitter" or "to become stubborn and obstinate" or "to feel left out." God says a person's shadow is either a home or a place where he feels rejected and left out; and as a result, he becomes stubborn and bitter about living in the shadow. However, a person abiding in the shadow never has to become bitter about being in the shadow.

The secret to feeling at home under the shadow is to dwell in the *secret place,* or to settle in, make it home, and then reap the wonderful benefits. Simply put, your shadow is either your home to which you run to for defense and security, or your shadow is where you feel left out, carry a grudge, feel bitter and angry, and desperately want to leave.

However, if you leave the shadow, you lose your security, your protection, your safety, your deliverance, your insight, your victory, and your promotion. God wants us to live under the shadow because of what is available to us in the shadows—security, protection, safety, deliverance, insight, victory, and promotion. But, a person has to make the decision for himself as to whether or not he is going to live in the shadow.

There are obvious blessings to living under the shadow, but exactly what is the shadow of the Almighty?

1. The shadow of the Almighty may be an occupation or a position that places you under another's authority or places you in their shadow. Many are in an occupation or a position where they live in another's shadow. For instance, a wife has been called to live in the shadow of her husband. A mother almost becomes like a servant to her children and often lives in the shadow of her children. Employees all work for another who might well have fame or who stands in the light as the leader. As the leader is in the light, he rightfully casts a shadow upon those who work for him. If those in the shadows are not careful, they will covet the place of light, nurture a grudge about being in the shadows, become bitter and resentful, and as a result, lose their security, their protection, their safety, their deliverance, their insight, their victory, and their promotion.

Our nation has suffered with people who do not want to be in the shadows. Our nation has watched a generation of women form organizations like the National Organization of Women (NOW) because of their resentment at being in the shadow. As a result, we have a nation of rebellious kids, homes without father figures, and troubled marriages. Why? Very simply put, women do not want to be under the protection of the shadow, and men do not want to cast a shadow.

Too many men want to put the woman in front, let her run the home, take care of the finances, and rear the children, while the men earn the money, turn over the paycheck, enjoy their buddies, and invest their time and energy in outdoor or sports-related activities. We need a nation of men who once again are willing to cast a shadow over their home and their family.

2. The shadow of the Almighty is a home, a church, or a school. I know of no other word more beautiful in our language than the word home. One of my favorite invitational songs is "Come home, come home, ye who are weary come home." I love home.

Many years ago numerous invitations began to come for me to go preach nearly every week in the summer. I soon realized that I was getting away from home too much. I was traveling all the time, and we had little children in our home. I found myself making statements to my family like, "Sometime we're going to spend some time together doing thus-and-so." I was even making statements to my wife like, "Honey, I love you, but I've got to go preach and do my part…" It suddenly occurred to me that I was running from the shadow of home; and quite honestly, I was letting others decide under which shadow I lived. I decided to choose under which shadow I would live; I chose home.

Many young people desperately want to get out of the house and be their own person. The young person who fulfills this wish loses his protection, his security, his safety, his deliverance, his insight, his victory, and his promotion. Sad to say, forsaking the shadow of the home, he usually takes the path of worldly living—no standards, no Bible reading, no prayer, no soul winning, and no church—and wakes up to find nothing—no shadow and no home. The young person who flippantly forsakes the shadow of his home will never know the joy of the shadow of home.

I live under the shadow of church. No Christian should ever let his schedule take him from underneath the shadow of the local church. The shadow of the local church is an authority every Christian needs in his life. A pastor casts a shadow over his church members. First Baptist Church casts a shadow of security, protection, safety, deliverance, insight, victory, and promotion for those who want to live under that shadow.

3. The shadow of the Almighty is an authority figure like a dad, a pastor, or a teacher. My shadow is the position of pastor of a local church. All authority figures—employer, police officer, principal—cast shadows that offer security, protection, safety, deliverance, insight, victory, and promotion.

4. The shadow of the Almighty might possibly be a grief or a sadness or a loss or a pain or a chronic illness. Heartbreak comes between you and the light of glory and hovers over you and puts you under the shadow which brings security, protection, safety, deliverance, insight, victory, and promotion!

Abiding under the shadow brings a myriad of benefits that every Christian can enjoy. However, with the benefits come lessons to be learned.

Every Christian needs to apply to his personal life the spiritual lessons he will learn by being under the shadow of the Almighty.

A. I want to learn to feel at home in the shadows. In Isaiah 53:3 the Bible says that Jesus was a man acquainted with grief. *"He is despised and rejected of men; a man of sorrows, and acquainted with grief; and we hid as it were our faces from him; he was despised, and we esteemed him not."* Jesus knew what it was like to live in the shadows; since He knew what it was like to live in the shadows, He decided to feel at home with the shadow. We must come to terms with our shadows and make friends with our shadows.

Teenagers need to make friends with their parents. A wife should make peace with her position as an occupant of her husband's shadow. A wife needs to thank God for the shadow He has provided for her. There is no higher occupation in the world than that of a wife and mother.

God oftentimes places a person in the shadow because he cannot succeed in the light. Out of kindness God removes some from the light and places them in the shadow to help them succeed, to find victory, to find honor, to find promotion, to find security, to find safety, and to find insight. God loves us so much He puts us in the shadow.

B. Your shadow is either your home to which you turn for refuge, or it is the place you feel left out or rejected. How sad it is when people just do not feel at home at home. Where does one go if he is not home at home? That is one reason why there are gangs. A gang is substitute shadow for the shadow of a home or a father or a local church.

C. I want to cast a shadow. Most people think they would be happier casting a shadow than living under a shadow. In fact, some people tried to cast their own shadow when they weren't supposed to cast a shadow.

• Absalom, David's son, prematurely cast a shadow when he felt his father wasn't doing his job as king. Six months later Absalom was hanging by his hair from a tree and casting a different kind of shadow on the ground with three darts in his heart.

• Cain wanted to cast his own shadow. He said, "God, You're not telling me what kind of sacrifices I give; I will not live under the shadow of Your rules." Exactly four verses after Cain murdered Abel, he cried out to God, "...*My punishment is greater than I can bear.*" (Genesis 4:13) So many people hated him that he fled to the land of Nod, "the land of wandering." Cain looked for himself and never found himself; he never felt at home anywhere because he would not live under the shadow of the rules of God.

• Adam and Eve were not content to know God; they wanted to be God. Obviously Adam and Eve could not cast a shadow like God could. As a result, their shadow cast the reproach and shame of sin all over mankind.

• Saul did not want to live in David's shadow. God was promoting David, and as the shadow of David grew, Saul became insanely jealous and tried to kill David. Ultimately, his senseless hatred cost him his life.

• Judas did not want to live in the shadow of Jesus and betrayed Him.

• Korah, Dathan, and Abiram decided not to sit in the shadow of their cousin Moses. God opened the ground and swallowed them as well as all of their relatives. God made the decision under whose shadow they would sit.

The happiest and most secure people in the world are those who make themselves comfortable under their own shadow.

They feel at home in the shadow.

**D. To live under a shadow, you must have a strong secret
life.** *"Thy word is a lamp unto my feet, and a light unto my path."*
(Psalm 119:105) The lack of a secret life makes a person feel
uncomfortable with living under the shadow. A person must
walk in the light—the Word of God—while living under the
shadow. Also, while we live in the shadows, we have a
Companion Who is light! Jesus Christ is the light of the world.
*"The LORD is my light and my salvation; whom shall I fear? The
LORD is the strength of my life; of whom shall I be afraid?"* (Psalm
27:1) Jesus is there to brighten the path of the people who have
been asked to live under the shadow. Those who are walking in
the light of the Scriptures and walking with the Jesus, Who is the
Light, have no problem walking under the shadow because it is
so bright they do not notice the shadow.

**E. An insecure person often attempts to create his own
light in order to cast his own shadow.** He is trying to be his own
man. In the shadow of God, the light one person casts is barely
significant. Those who try to cast a shadow are basically casting
an artificial light.

I met a teenage girl who arrogantly said, "Do you know **who**
you are talking to?"

I asked, "Who?"

"I've got my own gang," she bragged.

"Oh, I am so impressed," I countered. "I have my own gang
too. The difference is that my gang came from God, and your
gang is artificial light." That teenager was an insecure girl with
an insolent mouth, forward ways, and unscriptural tactics who
was looking for a mother to love her and a father who would
order her to stay home instead of letting her run the streets.
Insecure people are always trying to find their own light.

5. Those who cast a shadow must be sure to stand in God's light—not artificial light. Those who cry aloud behind the pulpits of America, who stand in front of Sunday school classrooms, who serve as deacons and bus workers, and who are moms and dads must stand in the light in which God has placed them. *"Jesus answered and said,…And I, if I be lifted up from the earth, will draw all men unto me."* (John 12:30, 32) Some tend to forget what draws people. A preacher who once magnified the truths of God starts teaching his own manmade principles and philosophies. That preacher has left the light, and in so doing, he has placed those who stand in his shadow in artificial light. Christians must magnify the Saviour and stand in His light.

6. We cast a shadow upon ourselves that is not of God; it is the shadow of sin. An individual casts this shadow upon himself as he tries to hide from the light of God. Sin is a self-made shadow that hides a person from God and prevents him from knowing God. Sad to say, a person who dies in the shadow of his own sins will live in the darkness of Hell forever. The moment a person trusts Christ as his Saviour, the shadows of sin are pushed away, and the light of the Gospel brings a glorious redemption and salvation to him. He trades the shadow of sin for a City of light!

CHAPTER EIGHT

I'LL USE MY BURDEN TO CARRY YOURS

"Brethren, if a man be overtaken in a fault, ye which are spiritual, restore such an one in the spirit of meekness; considering thyself, lest thou also be tempted. Bear ye one another's burdens, and so fulfil the law of Christ. For if a man think himself to be something, when he is nothing, he deceiveth himself. But let every man prove his own work, and then shall he have rejoicing in himself alone, and not in another. For every man shall bear his own burden."

(Galatians 6:1-5)

"For this thing I besought the Lord thrice, that it might depart from me. And he said unto me, My grace is sufficient for thee: for my strength is made perfect in weakness. Most gladly therefore will I rather glory in my infirmities, that the power of Christ may rest upon me. Therefore I take pleasure in infirmities, in reproaches, in necessities, in persecutions, in distresses for Christ's sake: for when I am weak, then am I strong." (II Corinthians 12:8-10)

LIVING A TRUTH BEGINS with understanding the truth. Once we understand the truth and grow to love it, then we desire to live that truth.

With that thought in mind, let's examine Galatians 6:2, which says, *"Bear ye one another's burdens, and so fulfil the law of Christ."* In verse 5, the bearing of burdens is addressed again, *"For every man shall bear his own burden."* I puzzled about these two verses for many years. Why am I first supposed to bear another person's burdens? Why shouldn't I first bear my own burdens? Once I have them under control and have learned how to bear burdens, would it not be logical for me then to bear another's burdens? Why would I practice on others to learn myself?

The order of these Scriptures is very important. God instructed that we first bear each other's burdens; then after we have borne each other's burdens, we are to turn our attention to our own burden.

Maturing in our Christian walk with Christ means helping to lift the burdens of others. Christian maturity is, quite simply, helping other people with their burdens. If only one word could summarize the Christian life, that word would be "others." Solving the problems and helping with the needs of others is the whole secret to the Christian life. "Others, Lord, yes, others, Let this my motto be / Help me to live for others, That I may live like Thee." "Others" was the motto by which Brother Hyles lived his life. Living for others, giving to others, and helping others are the marks of the Christian life.

Many of us have helped some people. We have lifted a wounded heart. We have helped a feeble person. We have been used to help carry another's load. We believe God is using us to help make a difference. However, very quickly we realize that we cannot help very many; we cannot help everyone who seeks our help. We soon become overwhelmed with all of the burdens of those who need our help. Frustration comes as we ask ourselves over and over, "How can I help them all?"

We seek counseling, we read all the books we can find about our burden, and we listen to every tape or CD on the subject. We just want to survive the coming hours. Why continue to cry out to God, "I can't even bear my own burdens! How am I supposed to help someone else's burden? God, please take away my burden so I can help others." It seems like the prayers fall on deaf ears, and we start questioning our relationship with God. "Why? Why? Why?"

Sometimes, humanly speaking, we just don't have all the answers to all the whys. I talked long distance to friends who had lost their third baby. When I asked my friend how he was doing, he said they had survived the first two miscarriages because they knew that God was in charge. He agonized, "But Brother Schaap, this is more than we can take! Is God judging us? Is God angry at us for some reason? Why is this happening over and over to us? I believe I already know the answer, but I just need to ask it. Why doesn't God seemingly want us to have children?"

I tried to reassure these good friends that God did indeed love them. My friend agreed with my pathetic reassurances and said, "I know, and Sunday I'll preach and tell the people that God is on the throne and that He is not judging us. But right now, my wife and I are crying our eyes out, and we feel very rejected by God."

Like my friends, you beg and plead, and nothing seems to happen. You nearly despair at the presence of your own burden. Your burden seems so much bigger and more cumbersome than the burdens of others. "God, why is my burden so big? I read my Bible every day, I fast and pray, I go to church every time the doors are open, I live for others, I work on a bus route, and I go soul winning. God, why don't You take my burden away?"

God doesn't answer.

How does God expect a person to carry his own burden and carry the burdens of others? The burdened person is barely making it on his own, but God still wants him to carry the burdens of others! What kind of a God does he serve? He feels like a spiritual cripple as he watches others effortlessly carrying their own heavy burdens and helping some others carry theirs at the same time. He wonders, "How in the world are they doing all that?" He desperately wants to serve God, and he wants to help others, but he is so afflicted with his own burden that it is interfering with all of his plans and desires. He pleads and begs for God to remove his burden, but God doesn't. He feels so abandoned by God.

"Is there no answer?" he wants to ask God, "Why did You give me a burden that keeps me from helping other people? I could have done so much more for others without that heartache. You have inhibited me from helping others. How can I follow Your command to bear another's burdens?"

If God tells us to bear one another's burdens, then He obviously provides us with the means of fulfilling His command. A person may already be limited in his ability to carry another's burdens, and seemingly when God gives him a burden of his own, He further limits this person's ability to carry others' burdens. No matter how much he complains about his burden, God is not going to take away that burden because His grace is sufficient! II Corinthians 12:9 says, *"And he said unto me, My grace is sufficient for thee: for my strength is made perfect in weakness."*

Paul asked God three times to take his burden. Three times God answered, "No!" because His grace was sufficient for Paul to carry his own burden as well as the burdens of others. What is that grace? Grace is using our personal burden to carry the burdens of others. The burdens get heavier, but we use our burden to carry others' burdens. God did not want to take Paul's burden; He provided Paul with a tool to live for others! God answered Paul's prayer and gave him a burden that would enable him to help even more people. Paul learned what a pleasure it was to carry the burdens of others!

When God gives a burden that seems too heavy to bear, He is also providing the tool for us to live for others. If we get rid of our burden, we cannot carry as many burdens as we could have if we had kept the burden God had tailor-made for us. We go to God and say, "God, please take my burden."

And God says, "No."

"But, God, I want to be used of You."

And God says, "I know."

"God, I can't be used of You with this burden."

And God says, "That is exactly how you're going to be used—with that burden."

What kind of burdens does God send? He lovingly sends grief and pain and chronic illness and heartache because that is the very tool He has chosen for us to use to carry the burdens of others. A person can carry many more burdens with his own burden than he can without his burden. A person's burden is really his burden bearer.

The question is—do you want to be used of God, or do you want Him to take away your burden? No one can have it both ways. The burden you have is the tool God gave you to help you live for Christ and to live for others. God's grace is sufficient for both. What is grace? Grace is using your burden to carry the burdens of others.

Job used his burden of multiple heartbreaks to help others with their burdens. David wrote a book to help others with their burdens. Mrs. Marlene Evans used her burden of cancer to help others; she wrote books to help others in their struggle with a chronic illness. Some with long-term chronic problems have one of the greatest potentials to be used of God; they have a burden bearer. Those with chronic problems, chronic illnesses, chronic financial difficulties, and chronic relationship problems ought to be envied because their problems are tools to bear the burdens of others. Stop fighting the burden God has given you and use it to bear the burdens of others. You will live for others when you accept the burden God has given you.

CHAPTER NINE

BLESSED ARE THOSE WHO GET THE WIND KNOCKED OUT OF THEM

"Blessed are the poor in spirit: for their's is the kingdom of heaven." (Matthew 5:3)

THE MESSAGE OF THE beatitudes was primarily given for the benefit of the disciples of Christ. A disciple of Christ is a follower of Christ, one who has disciplined himself to follow Christ, and one who has said, "I want to have Christ be my pattern for living."

The word *blessed* means "truly fortunate, happy." The word *poor* means "absolute poverty—bereft of everything one has." The message of Matthew 5:3 is "Fortunate, happy, supremely blessed, well-off are those who are in absolute poverty, bankrupt, begging, who have been robbed of the spiritual wind of their life," or "Blessed are those who get the wind knocked out of them."

When my son was a little tyke about four or five years of age, he loved to play football and wrestle with me. One day he decided to embark on a boxing career and said, "Come on, Dad! Let's box!"

I thought, "No way is a four year old going to hurt me." My defenses were down, and my son drew back and punched me right in the nose. It hurt! Without thinking and by reflex, I punched him back in the stomach. He fell on the floor, and big tears began to run down his face. When he finally caught his breath, he said, "Dad, I couldn't breathe!" What happened to Kenny is what God is saying in Matthew 5:3. "Christian, aren't you fortunate when you are so paralyzed that you have no resources of your own?"

Why are we fortunate and what could be so blessed about being knocked down spiritually? The truth is that God just does not see things the way we humans see them. We see things through a glass darkly. We see things in reflection of how we, our family, our friends, and acquaintances interpret them. God says, "When you are knocked down and bereft of your dependence upon unspiritual things and when you have no place to turn but to Me, that is when you are really well-off!"

What could be so blessed about a cancer report? What could be so fortunate about a terrible disease? What could be so fortunate about the death of a loved one? What is so blessed about a wayward child who has broken his parents' hearts? What is so fortunate about problems that make a person feel like he got kicked in the stomach and like his breath is knocked out of him? Why would God call that being happy? Quite simply, God's purposes are very different than ours.

When the last chapter of Job was written, not one time did God apologize to him. God did not apologize for taking his health or for killing his children or for putting him in misery with boils on his body, or for his friends' forsaking of him, or for his wife's seemingly turning her back on him. God never apologized because all that happened to Job is exactly what God intended for him.

When David was hiding from Saul in the cave of Adullam with 600 followers, God never apologized to David for the trouble that He brought to him. Rather, He had David write a book of praises to help those who have the wind knocked out of them.

God never apologized to Ezekiel for killing his wife, and the morning of her death, God required the unthinkable—He said, "Don't even shed a tear for her." God never apologized for asking His prophet to do that hard thing. God never apologized to Paul for giving him a thorn in the flesh. Neither will God apologize to you for the cancer you have growing in your body. God will not apologize to you for pain or suffering or tribulation. Why? It is when the wind is knocked out of us that we most realize how much we need Him.

What is the blessing of an individual who knows that he desperately needs God? *"…Their's is the kingdom of heaven."* That Scripture means that everything in the kingdom of Heaven is ours!

1. **The kingdom of Heaven is the wealth of Heaven.** All of Heaven's wealth is available to the poor in spirit. Those who are bankrupt in spirit have available to them Heaven's streets of solid gold!

2. **The kingdom of Heaven is the angelic warriors of Heaven.** Not only do the poor in spirit have access to Heaven's wealth, but they also have the angelic armies of Heaven on their side. As I consider the blessedness of knowing Heaven's armies are at my call, I am reminded of a thrilling account I read in a book of World War II stories. For the epic December 1944 Battle of the Bulge, Hitler kept some of his best troops in reserve, and

he launched a strategic campaign that plunged deep into the Allied offensive fronts in France. As a result of that masterful stratagem, our American solider boys almost lost that crucial battle. Hitler's troops pushed a huge bulge into the frontal assault line and almost cut off troops from reinforcements. Had his armies succeeded in that incursion, more than likely the Germans would have won the war, or at the very least, delayed the end of the war.

I read an account about a sergeant and a handful of survivors in his company who were dug in a trench. They received word that the Germans were advancing, and their orders were to hold their position at all cost. One of those soldier boys was a Christian, and when he heard the standing orders, he began to pray, "Oh God, You have to help us stop these Germans. God, if You don't help us, we've lost the war."

Sure enough, it wasn't long before they heard the advance of the German troops with their tanks. When the Americans resisted, the Germans called for a bombardment of their position. The smoke of the battlefield began to rise, and the screams of the wounded could be heard above the sound of gunfire and exploding grenades and shells. The entrenched under-strength company of American soldiers knew they had no chance against a thousand advancing Germans. They knew their position would soon be overrun by the enemy, not to mention that their ammunition was almost gone.

When the advancing Germans were about a thousand yards away, their forward movement ceased. For no apparent reason, no more shots were fired; quiet reigned on the battleground. The Americans huddled together in their trenches, making plans for the next onslaught. The sergeant cautioned them to use their ammunition sparingly. "We may die, but we are going to die taking a lot of Germans with us," he said. He changed positions to scan the battlefield.

To his shock and consternation, he saw three German officers waving a white flag, advancing toward their position. In broken English they repeatedly shouted, "We surrender. American, we surrender."

Rightfully so, the Americans thought it was a trick, but the sergeant cautiously left his trench to meet with the officers. Only he knew that about a dozen soldiers remained, so he asked, "Why do you want to surrender?"

"My men won't fight anymore," an officer explained. "Your soldiers are unlike any soldiers we have ever seen."

Of course, the sergeant didn't have any idea about whom the officer was referring. "Tell me about them," he said.

"They were ten feet tall, with flaming swords and shields. My troops are terrified! We want to surrender; we cannot fight your warriors from Heaven."

The unsaved sergeant still had no idea what the German officer meant, but the Christian soldier boy knew! He knew God had heard his battlefield prayer and that the armies of Heaven had been dispatched to help a handful of weary soldiers stop the encroachment of the German army. Those armies stood guard as that handful of Americans marched a thousand German troops into a POW camp!

Blessed are those who are outnumbered a thousand to ten! Blessed are those Christians who are outnumbered by the armies of Hell because the armies of Heaven are on their side!

3. **The kingdom of Heaven is the glory of Heaven.** The songwriter wrote, "Heaven came down and glory filled my soul."

4. **The kingdom of Heaven is the music of Heaven.** *"And he hath put a new song in my mouth, even praise unto our God...."*

(Psalm 40:3) When the days get long and weary, a song can bring consolation in the night.

Blessed is the man who has no place to turn except to God because that man has the kingdom of Heaven with him! However, some who are vanquished in spirit never avail themselves of all that the kingdom of Heaven offers. To be quite frank, they seem quite miserable and unhappy. These people seem lost in their personal valley of grief and depression. Why?

Why do some stay in the valley when the kingdom of Heaven is so available? Quite simply because those caught in the throes of grief and depression have not longed for and hungered for Heaven's kingdom, and that is the most heartbreaking grief of all for the greatest thing about the kingdom of Heaven is the King!

If Christ is our life, we don't have to live a miserable existence. If we have Christ, we are rich and have more than enough. He will never leave us or forsake us! No matter who leaves us, who quits, who dies, or who walks out, we are blessed because we will always have the King!

Blessed is the man who, when he has lost all that he can lose on this earth, realizes he cannot lose the kingdom of Heaven. When a person has lost all of his earthly wealth, he has access to Heaven's wealth. When he has lost his physical health, he has a new body waiting in Heaven. When he has lost all his earthly friends, he has *"...a friend that sticketh closer than a brother."* (Proverbs 18:24) When he is attacked and reviled and persecuted, he has the army of Heaven on his side.

Blessed is the man who has the spiritual wind knocked out of him. Blessed is the man when pain and misery and sadness and sickness come. Blessed is the man when responsibility larger than life looms on the horizon. Blessed is the man when all Hell assails him. Blessed is the man when the world of the flesh and the Devil assaults him. Blessed is the man who realizes that this world is not his home because he knows the kingdom of Heaven, the wealth of Heaven, the glory of Heaven, the armies of Heaven, the music of Heaven, and the King of Heaven will be his! There is no better news than that!

CHAPTER TEN

THE TRIAL
OF BITTER WATER

"Speak unto the children of Israel, and say unto them, If any man's wife go aside, and commit a trespass against him, And a man lie with her carnally, and it be hid from the eyes of her husband, and be kept close, and she be defiled, and there be no witness against her, neither she be taken with the manner; And the spirit of jealousy come upon him, and he be jealous of his wife, and she be defiled: or if the spirit of jealousy come upon him, and he be jealous of his wife, and she be not defiled." (Numbers 5:12-14)

THE TRIAL OF BITTER water, as Numbers chapter 5 is called, involved a man who suspected that his wife had been unfaithful to him. The husband took his wife to the priest and forced her to go through a proving time. In Old Testament times, she really had no choice. She was placed on a chair that faced the tabernacle, or the presence of God. The priest prepared a drink with water and some dust from the floor of the tabernacle. Mixing the dust and water created a muddy flurry she was required to hold while the priest placed his hand on her head and pronounced a curse or a blessing on her. The wife drank the solution, and then they waited for God's judgment or curse. If the wife was guilty of infidelity, she developed an extremely horrific disease and then suffered the consequences of that disease. *"Be not deceived; God is not mocked: for whatsoever a man soweth, that shall he also reap."* (Galatians 6:7) The whole nation of Israel would know that this wife was guilty of a hidden sin—infidelity. On the other hand, if she was innocent, she would give birth to a baby and become a free woman. The whole nation would know that her husband had no grounds for his charge of adultery.

Whether the wife was guilty or innocent, she had to drink the bitter water, and she had to bear the ignominy of everyone's watching. Just like this woman faced the trial of bitter water, on the menu of life there is some bitter water. Nobody goes through life unscathed. Not one person goes through life without a sudden reality check— a sudden unexpected event that has the power to permanently change one's life for better or for worse.

While one family invites guests for food and fellowship to commemorate a graduation or a wedding, another family invites guests for food and fellowship following the burial of a loved one. On the same day that a happy 16 year old receives his driver's license, grief comes to a teenager who just wrecked the family car. As one farmer rejoices for the sun that grows his crops, another curses the sun that withers his crops. Likewise, one gardener prays for the rain to nourish his vegetables, and another curses the skies that unleash the deluge that has destroyed his garden. The obvious tension of opposites in life is vital to the sustenance of that life. Just like two teams play tug of war, there is tension in life.

For example, there is a tension of learning and a tension of testing, a tension of inhaling and a tension of exhaling, a tension of the windup and the tension of the delivery, a tension of the backswing and the forward swing, rest and work, faith and sight, riches and poverty, health and sickness, and an ebb and a flow. One cannot merely inhale, windup, backward swing, rest, faith, riches, health, ebb, and learn all of the time. One also has to exhale, deliver, forward swing, work, sight, poverty, sickness, flow, and be tested. The constant tension must be present; they are complements to each other.

In the trial of bitter water, the wife accused of infidelity felt the tension of innocence, and she likewise felt the tension of accusation. Whether there was guilt or innocence, right or wrong, the tension was still there. No matter how hard a Christian prays, reads his Bible, or how well he lives his life, the tests of life will come. These sudden dramatic changes in the pathway of life will cause him to question, "What happened?"

Some important lessons about life can be drawn from Numbers chapter 5 concerning the tension every Christian encounters on the playing field of life.

1. **A life of faith requires a certain amount of tension.** The Greek root word for faith, *pestos*, comes from a word that means "tension" or "taut." The greater a person's faith, the greater the tautness or tension! Men of great faith live under tremendous tension. The more tension a Christian feels in life, the greater the opportunity God will put before him. A life of faith is a state of tension, and tension is good.

2. **Tension keeps us within set boundaries.** Picture a tug of war game between two teams. If one team quits pulling, the opposing side can take their heretofore opponents anywhere they desire. They can be taken from the boundaries of the playing field. With no tautness or tension, a person is free to roam anywhere he wants to go, even to the point of leaving the will of God and leaving the place of God's service. Why? Because there

is no tension pulling on the other side. Tension is important! Even harmful tension is a reminder for a Christian to stay within the boundaries God has placed in his life.

In Bible days, every wife knew if infidelity came in her life, she could be brought before the Lord for testing. This knowledge kept a wife fairly pure. That tension that would come kept her from walking outside her boundaries.

3. Tests and tension of life are bitter to every person. Going through a test of life tastes bitter to everyone. The innocent woman had to drink the bitter water even though she was pure and clean and proper. The water tasted just as bitter to the woman who was immoral and guilty of infidelity.

Having reality checks bring bitterness to everyone. There are no **sweet** sudden changes. When a godly Christian loses a spouse, that is bitter; when a wicked person loses a spouse, that is bitter. Bitter events are bitter to everyone.

4. Tests and tension expose a person's strengths and weaknesses. No doubt the innocent woman who was forced to drink the bitter water wondered why no one believed in her innocence. The bitter water test merely confirmed whether she was innocent of or exposed in her guilt. God allows the tests of life to come in our lives. When the sudden shockwave of emotional trials collide with your calm, tranquil way of life, suddenly you are forced to expose to the world what you really are. Are you strong or weak? Lest you think God has it in for you, He put His own Son on the cross and let Him be exposed.

The tests of life reveal an inner man's strengths and weaknesses. For example, nearly every military hero was first a combat hero. He fought in a war and rose through the ranks of the enlisted. If there had been no World War II, probably the strengths of soldiers like General Dwight D. Eisenhower, General

George Patton, and General Douglas MacArthur would never have been brought to the forefront. More than likely, they would have just been good men who attended a military academy and did well in their class. But the strife, tension, clash, conflict, and tension of war allowed men to expose their strengths.

War also exposes its cowards. Most of those who quit the military academy and never finish anything worthwhile in life are never heard about, but everyone recognizes the names of Benedict Arnold and Adolph Hitler. Just as war and conflict expose great men, they also expose those who are weak.

Strife is necessary in life. Strife enables God to show an individual what he is doing and what he is really like. Sometimes a person lives in such an oblivious, glazed existence, surrounded by an artificial cocoon, that he is unwilling to let God show him what he is really like. God sometimes has to force that person to look into a mirror by means of emotional circumstances so that his inner being can be revealed. Sudden or stressful events reveal the inner truths of every person.

5. When bitter experiences cause one to become bitter, he proves to his accusers that their assumptions were correct. A person angrily shakes his fist at God because of the proving tests of life. Attentive onlookers are more interested in how he reacts than to the real facts; in their eyes, those kinds of actions declare a person's guilt more than his innocence.

One of the major television networks in Chicago called the church and asked me to grant an interview about a certain event that took place in Northwest Indiana. I agreed to an interview. When the reporter came, he brought a cameraman with him. As he walked into my office, he stated that they were going to set up their equipment for a live feed. I explained that I would not be going on television. The reporter argued that he needed to get my reaction to that certain situation. I informed him that I did not deal with sensationalism. "We both are interested in the truth," I explained. "However, you are more interested in truth—good or bad—that is sensational. I'm only interested in good truth that helps."

He tried one last ploy, "But Reverend, the public needs to hear your opinion."

I said, "My own church people do not want to hear my opinion; they hired me to bring them the truth of God's Word. The community doesn't even know who Jack Schaap is, and they do not want to hear my opinion. You want reaction, and I don't live in reaction. If you have a question to ask me, I'll respond."

"I don't have any questions," he said.

I could not believe he came to an interview without any questions written down! I have been interviewed by junior high-age yearbook people who have more experience than he did. Obviously no interview took place. How some people rise to important positions is beyond me!

Like this television reporter, most people are only into reaction, and the wrong kind of reaction can be interpreted as guilt when there is no guilt.

6. Bitter experiences usually cause friends and loved ones to pull away from the one who is being tested. In Psalm 38:11 David said, *"My lovers and my friends stand aloof from my sore; and my kinsmen stand afar off."* The bitter wound that came to David caused his friends and loved ones to distance themselves from him. David needed desperately to have a friend at this time in his life.

When a person goes through the troubling, life-changing events of life, those people on whom he thought he could count are the ones who will most probably withdraw from him and then watch for his reaction. Most people decide whether or not to stand with a loved one by how he reacts to the troubling times in life. They want to watch how he handles the isolation of when it's just him, his problem, and God. David said in Psalm 38:15, *"For in thee, O LORD, do I hope: thou wilt hear, O Lord my God."* Some who are tested repeatedly keep a sweet spirit, and God overwhelms them with an army of friends and loved ones.

That is what people loved about Brother Hyles. Through the years when this ministry faced the tests of life, Brother Hyles led the people to react properly. The proper reaction drew people like a magnet because people want to be associated with heroes. **A hero is someone who has succeeded while struggling with the same problems others use as excuses for their failures.**

Feeling isolated and alone during one of life's testing times is a natural biblical principle. People will watch from a distance until they discover what a man's true character reveals. If they see a display of bitterness or anger, they will probably withdraw completely. Call them Pharisees, fake friends, or pseudo friends, the bottom line is that the bitter spirit caused them to distance themselves.

Personally, I don't have a lot of confidence that people will stay faithful to me when I am under pressure, but I have confidence that real men of God will come back when they see the true character exposed.

7. **Bitter experiences cause some to become corrupt and others to become clean.** The one who goes through a bitter experience and stumbles becomes bitter and exposes himself as a weak character who could not take pressure. Often, that one who falls points an accusing finger at others and blames them for his bitter condition. On the other hand, those who pass the test of bitter water find personal freedom and increased productivity.

8. The one who fails the test of bitter water becomes a curse to himself and to his family. When parents (or a parent) become bitter over a trial in life and never recover, their bitterness is often acted out in their children. The children will bear that animosity and deal with it for the rest of their lives because their parents were not strong enough to set the proper example when the bad times came. *"Finally, my brethren, be strong in the Lord, and in the power of his might."* (Ephesians 6:10)

Nobody goes through life unscathed. Everyone has bitter water experiences. No matter what life brings, we can say with Job, *"For I know that my redeemer liveth."* (Job 19:25a) The bad times came for Job, and he never allowed bitterness to rule his life. When the testing times come, people either get bitter or better; make sure, like Job of old, you get better.

CHAPTER ELEVEN

IF YOU WANT TO BE AN OVERCOMER, YOU MUST LEARN TO OVERCOME

"Unto the angel of the church of Ephesus write; These things saith he that holdeth the seven stars in his right hand, who walketh in the midst of the seven golden candlesticks; I know thy works, and thy labour, and thy patience, and how thou canst not bear them which are evil: and thou hast tried them which say they are apostles, and are not, and hast found them liars: And hast borne, and hast patience, and for my name's sake hast laboured, and hast not fainted. Nevertheless I have somewhat against thee, because thou hast left thy first love. Remember therefore from whence thou art fallen, and repent, and do the first works; or else I will come unto thee quickly, and will remove thy candlestick out of his place, except thou repent. But this thou hast, that thou hatest the deeds of the Nicolaitanes, which I also hate. He that hath an ear, let him hear what the Spirit saith unto the churches; To him that overcometh will I give to eat of the tree of life, which is in the midst of the paradise of God." (Revelation 2:1-7)

In the book of Revelation, seven brief letters were written to cities with churches, and these churches were representative churches of all churches. I personally believe that any one church can go through all seven representations. At times a church endures a time of persecution like the church at Smyrna. Sometimes the church is like Philadelphia, a young, aggressive, zealous church that grows in leaps and bounds. The church of Ephesus was an established, organized church that had forgotten its zeal and enthusiasm. At times a church is as the church at Pergamos where it goes through a time of perhaps a little backsliding and wavers. These seven churches of Revelation are like snapshots of any church at any particular time in its history.

Seven times in Revelation the Bible talks about overcoming. Revelation 2:7 says, "*He that hath an ear, let him hear what the Spirit saith unto the churches;* **To him that overcometh** *will I give to eat of the tree of life, which is in the midst of the paradise of God.*"

Revelation 2:11, "*He that hath an ear, let him hear what the Spirit saith unto the churches;* **He that overcometh** *shall not be hurt of the second death.*"

Revelation 2:17, "*He that hath an ear, let him hear what the Spirit saith unto the churches;* **To him that overcometh** *will I give to eat of the hidden manna, and will give him a white stone, and in the stone a new name written, which no man knoweth saving he that receiveth it.*"

Revelation 2:26, "*And* **he that overcometh**, *and keepeth my works unto the end, to him will I give power over the nations.*"

Revelation 3:5, "**He that overcometh**, *the same shall be clothed in white raiment; and I will not blot out his name out of the book of life, but I will confess his name before my Father, and before his angels.*"

Revelation 3:12, "**Him that overcometh** *will I make a pillar in the temple of my God, and he shall go no more out: and I will write upon him the name of my God, and the name of the city of my God, which is new Jerusalem, which cometh down out of heaven from my God: and I will write upon him my new name.*"

Revelation 3:21, "**To him that overcometh** *will I grant to sit with me in my throne, even as I also overcame, and am set down with my Father in his throne.*"

Quite simply, the Bible is saying if you want to be an overcomer, you must learn to overcome. Many people really want to live the victorious Christian life, but they do not want to fight any battles and experience any victories. That is impossible. To be an overcomer, lessons must be learned about overcoming.

The victorious Christian is called an overcomer, and God makes many special promises to overcomers. In Heaven, overcomers will be set apart, and they will be the recipients of much that will be desired.

1. Overcomers will receive special meals in Heaven.
2. Overcomers will receive special positions of authority.
3. Overcomers will receive a special wardrobe.
4. Overcomers will receive a special showplace of honor with Jesus Christ and His Father. Jesus will personally introduce an overcomer to His Father.
5. Overcomers will receive special personalized gifts. I enjoy using a beautiful pen with my name engraved on it that was given to me by two staff ladies. Likewise, personalized gifts like my pen are waiting in Heaven for overcomers.
6. Overcomers will enjoy special reserved box seats where they will watch all the events from that vantage place in Heaven.
7. Overcomers will receive a special inheritance. An over-

comer will receive twice as much as is given to anyone—like the firstborn in the Old Testament received a double portion.

Would you like to be an overcomer—one of the ones who receives all seven of these special privileges when he gets to Heaven? The way might not be easy because overcomers conquer whatever God puts in front of them.

1. An overcomer is the one who conquers that one unique struggle or testing which has been the most difficult for him to conquer. Each of the churches in Revelation struggled with something different they had yet to overcome. Revelation 2:4, *"Nevertheless I have somewhat against thee, because thou hast left thy first love."* The church at Ephesus had to overcome a "love-life" problem. Their love had grown sophisticated, cold, and arrogant. Jesus wanted them to return to the zealous, affectionate, passionate love they once had for Him.

Revelation 2:9 and 10a, *"I know thy works, and tribulation, and poverty, (but thou art rich) and I know the blasphemy of them which say they are Jews, and are not, but are the synagogue of Satan. Fear none of those things...."* The Christians at Smyrna were being betrayed to the government, suffering persecution, and being martyred. Jesus did not want them to buckle under the pressure of persecution.

Revelation 2:14, *"But I have a few things against thee, because thou hast there them that hold the doctrine of Balaam, who taught Balac to cast a stumblingblock before the children of Israel, to eat things sacrificed unto idols, and to commit fornication."* The church at Pergamos was married to the world. *Pergamos* means "marriage." The church at Thyatira needed to be purged of immoral leadership. In the church at Sardis, the people were living in the past and doing nothing in the present. The church at Philadelphia was a weak church and barely had enough strength to do anything. The Laodiceans were lukewarm, didn't have any zeal, and had no desire to grow.

An overcomer vanquishes his personal problem—that one area that is so difficult to change in his life. That struggle might be his marriage difficulties, jealousy, anger or strife, a hot temper, a lack of zeal, an unChristian spirit, or undisciplined character. Every person knows his personal unique problem that he needs to overcome.

A person does not become an overcomer because he conquers another's problem. He can only be an overcomer if he conquers his own personal problem. What is your besetting sin? Conquer it! There should be nothing in a person's heart or thinking that would make him want to ever say or admit, "I just couldn't conquer that." When I get to Heaven, I want to shout, "I overcame it!" A Christian must come to the point in his life where he decides to overcome that besetting sin. He must keep on struggling and fighting it until he overcomes it. Declare war on that one thing that keeps you from being an overcomer in Heaven someday!

No one wants to get to Heaven and say, "I would have been an overcomer except for...." Personally, I do not want any exceptions in my life. Nearly everyone wants to have exceptions, so the exceptional person is the one who has no exceptions. Too many people say, "I would have been a great one too, except...." God has given everyone the grace, the tools, and the power to overcome his besetting sin and to be called an overcomer. It is not enough to conquer others' weaknesses; it is not enough to conquer or resist a common temptation. You must conquer **your** temptation, and until you conquer yours, you will never be an overcomer.

"I know thy works, and thy labour, and thy patience, and how

thou canst not bear them which are evil: and thou hast tried them which say they are apostles, and are not, and hast found them liars: And hast borne, and hast patience, and for my name's sake hast laboured, and hast not fainted." (Revelation 2:2) These church members at Ephesus did a lot of good; however, none of their personal work made them an overcomer. Why? Because the area on which they needed to work was their love life. They tried to excuse their lack of love by their hard work and their discerning spirit. However, becoming an overcomer means looking at your weakness, not your strengths.

Too many have polished their strengths to a high gloss, all the while ignoring their weaknesses. That is why the problem areas in their lives need constant attention. Refusing to deal with that one besetting issue is their weakness.

2. Being an overcomer implies a strong adversary. When we get to Heaven, God will not give us any reward for conquering that which never was a problem to us. The ability of one's adversary determines whether or not God calls you an overcomer. God doesn't judge by what **you** call a tough adversary. For example, God is not going to give an award for overcoming nicotine to someone who has never smoked. That award is for someone who has been struggling with tobacco dependence for years and years. The person who was never interested in rock 'n' roll will not receive an overcomer award for hating rock music. However, when someone who grew up in that environment and attended rock concerts gives up that culture and lives for the Lord Jesus Christ, God sees him as an overcomer. For that person, the rock music culture was a strong adversary.

The one who has never tasted liquor will not get an overcomer award for giving up alcoholic beverages. The one who has been addicted to the bottle is the one who wins the award for overcoming a besetting sin–alcoholism.

When facing some kind of temptation in life, the more demanding the adversary one faces, the greater the opportunity to be genuinely called an overcomer in Heaven. An overcomer does not buckle when the problems get tough.

Stand erect like John Paul Jones stood on the deck of the *Bonhomme Richard* when the captain of the *Serapis* asked for his surrender, knowing his ship was sinking from the cannon barrages of the English and shout, "I have not yet begun to fight!" When the captain of the *Serapis* asked for his surrender, Jones rammed the *Serapis* with the *Bonhomme Richard*, boarded the enemy ship, conquered the enemy in hand-to-hand combat, received their surrender, and watched the *Bonhomme Richard* sink into the dark Atlantic seas. John Paul Jones proved that courage and determination could overcome all odds. The *Serapis* was a better ship than the *Bonhomme Richard*; it was newer, faster, and had more guns. However, the captain of the *Serapis* did not count on the nature of a well- disciplined crew who would overcome the *Bonhomme Richard*'s disadvantages of being older, smaller, and slower.

Learn what it means to fight. Don't be afraid to get scraped, bruised, and bloodied spiritually. When failure comes, get back up with blood dripping and shins bruised and say, "I think I'm just beginning to get angry enough to really start fighting!" Defeating the adversary means you have the privilege and opportunity to be called an overcomer.

3. Overcoming is a personal struggle. The Bible says, *"Him that overcometh,"* not "they who overcome." Sin is usually a group event; righteousness is always a singular event. I like personal victory in the Christian life. Jesus went to the cross alone, He died alone, He was buried alone, and He arose alone. That is a picture of how a person overcomes—all by his lonesome with the help of God. Too many are looking for others to have the overcoming victory for them. **We** are not overcomers; **you** are going to overcome.

There is a formula for overcoming. In all seven of Revelation's short letters, the same statement was repeated: *"He that hath an ear, let him hear."* In fact, it is the most repeated statement by the Lord Jesus Christ in all of His sayings in the Bible. Fifteen times Jesus said, *"He that hath an ear, let him **hear**."* The greatest commandment in the entire Bible is, *"**Hear, O Israel**."* What is the formula for being an overcomer?

1. Listen. If every person would just listen to the preaching and listen to the Spirit as he reads the Bible, he would have all the answers he needed. The one who listens learns.

2. Learn it. In all seven letters to the churches, Jesus said, "Remember what you heard and learn it." Probably 99 percent know exactly what the answers are, they just don't want to learn it. The truth of the matter is, if most people took a quiz on how to have a happy marriage or how to rear a happy family or how to be a good Christian, they would pass the test.

3. Live it. God wants us to hold fast, to be faithful to the end, to not let go, and to keep on. Revelation 12:11, *"And they overcame him by the blood of the Lamb, and by the word of their testimony...."* Your testimony is your living the truth year after year after year until you are characterized by that truth.

An overcomer is someone who listens, learns it, lives it, and never stops living it. He reads his Bible, reads his Bible, reads his Bible, and dies reading his Bible. He prays and never stops praying, and prays without ceasing.

Many years ago I was walking through the shopping mall with Kenny who was just a little three-year-old boy. The store was closing, and our car was parked at the far end of the mall. It was a cold night, so I didn't want to walk outside. I said, "Hang on," as I started walking faster and faster.

"Daddy," he said, "my little leggies just can't keep up with your big, long legs."

He finally grabbed a hold of my leg, and I "dragged" him through the mall. Every now and then I asked, "Are you still with me?"

"Daddy, I'm still hangin' on, and I'm never lettin' go!"

It seems like everyone likes to try "hangin' on" for a little while, but those who are overcomers continue to do it through the end of their life. If you want to be an overcomer, you need to hang on and never let go!

CHAPTER TWELVE

I WILL LEAVE OFF
MY HEAVINESS

"Though I were perfect, yet would I not know my soul: I would despise my life. This is one thing, therefore I said it, He destroyeth the perfect and the wicked. If the scourge slay suddenly, he will laugh at the trial of the innocent. The earth is given into the hand of the wicked: he covereth the faces of the judges thereof; if not, where, and who is he? Now my days are swifter than a post: they flee away, they see no good. They are passed away as the swift ships: as the eagle that hasteth to the prey. If I say, I will forget my complaint, I will leave off my heaviness, and comfort myself: My soul is weary of my life; I will leave my complaint upon myself; I will speak in the bitterness of my soul." (Job 9:21-27, 10:1)

THE BOOK OF JOB and Job's life allow Christians to have an incredible panoramic view into the life of a man of God who had every reason to be depressed, who became very depressed, and then came out of that depression. The word *heaviness* in Job 9:27 is a fitting biblical word describing what is now termed "depression." Heaviness is always associated with a melancholy soul or a depressed spirit. A very heavy weight pulls and drags down the soul deeper and deeper just like an emotional gravity. Today's word *depression* has that same connotation.

The holiday seasons—especially Christmas and New Year's—and the following weeks are usually described by psychologists and psychiatrists as some of the most depressing times of the year. In the Tuesday, January 11, 2005, Gary, Indiana, *Post Tribune*, an article entitled, "What's Happening Outside Affects Us on the Inside," stated, "The transition from autumn to winter, and even from early winter to the bitter, post-holiday winter, is an especially tough time for many people. As the days get shorter, lack of sunlight is a contributing factor to seasonal affective disorder, or SAD. It is estimated that 6 percent of the population suffers from winter depression, and as many as 20 percent might have a milder form." SAD peaks during January and February.

Certainly not everyone is affected by the holiday blues or with SAD, but both wreak havoc in the lives of many people. In a person's youth, generally the holidays are associated with delightful times. Unfortunately for many, depression comes as a result of being off schedule, of eating too many sweets, of gaining unnecessary pounds, and of trying to be the mediator in hurtful situations such as divorce. Many reasons exist for depression's entering into the arena of one's life.

If anyone had reason to be depressed, the man Job did. He experienced the loss of all of his wealth, of all of his co-workers and employees, of his ten children, and of his good health. What he suffered reminds me of what many experienced on September 11, 2001, with the World Trade Center disaster, with the sudden loss of so many without any warning.

In Job chapter 10, Job was very descriptive about his feelings and about his personal heaviness of spirit.

1. *"My soul is weary of my life."* (verse 1) Job was tired of living.

2. *"I will speak in the bitterness of my soul."* (verse 1) Emotionally and physically, Job had a bitter taste in his soul and heart.

3. *"I will say unto God, Do not condemn me; shew me wherefore thou contendest with me."* (verse 2) Job felt God was angry at him. Job longed for God to reveal the problem so he could confess and go on with his life.

4. *"Hast thou eyes of flesh? or seest thou as man seeth? Are thy days as the days of man? are thy years as man's days."* (verses 4, 5) Job was saying that God could not possibly understand how he felt; after all, God was a spirit and not made of flesh.

5. *"Thine hands have made me and fashioned me together round about; yet thou dost destroy me."* (verse 8) Job felt like God was letting him be destroyed—for no reason at all!

6. *"And these things hast thou hid in thine heart: I know that this is with thee."* (verse 13) Job realized that God knew how was he was suffering, but Job did not understand why God did nothing to alleviate the suffering.

7. *"If I sin, then thou markest me, and thou wilt not acquit me from mine iniquity. If I be wicked, woe unto me; and if I be righteous, yet will I not lift up my head. I am full of confusion; therefore see thou mine affliction."* (verses 14, 15) Job was tempted to sin as a way of escaping his misery—if only temporarily. He knew that if he sinned, he was giving God a good reason to bring suffering into his life; but if he was doing was right, God was still allowing him to be tormented. Job was very confused.

8. *"For it increaseth. Thou huntest me as a fierce lion: and again thou shewest thyself marvellous upon me. Thou renewest thy witnesses against me, and increasest thine indignation upon me; changes and*

war are against me." (verses 16, 17) Job felt that the more he talked to God about his situation, the worse his condition became. God had seemingly distanced himself from Job—for no good reason.

9. *"Wherefore then hast thou brought me forth out of the womb? Oh that I had given up the ghost, and no eye had seen me! I should have been as though I had not been; I should have been carried from the womb to the grave."* (verses 18, 19) In his great anguish, Job wished he had never been born.

10. *"Are not my days few? cease then, and let me alone, that I may take comfort a little."* (verse 20) Job felt the best thing God could do for him was to leave him alone in his depression.

11. *"Before I go whence I shall not return, even to the land of darkness and the shadow of death; A land of darkness, as darkness itself; and of the shadow of death, without any order, and where the light is as darkness."* (verses 21, 22) Job was convinced that God was going to let him die in his wretched condition. Job definitely had some legitimate reasons to be heavy of spirit.

Depression is a fact of life for everyone, and depression is precipitated by singular events in the life of each individual. The death of a loved one often brings depression. Imagine Job's anguish over losing all ten children in one cataclysmic event. The loss of good health and the subsequent days of searching for answers and the days of recuperation often bring depression. Historians believe that Job's pain came as a result of the excruciating disease of elephantiasis. No doubt if Job were alive in the twenty-first century, most certainly his loss of good health would have been diagnosed as being stress related. The cure would have been meted in a respectable form such as Prozac or valium or morphine.

The book of Job is a textbook case to teach us about our own emotions and feelings and how to deal with them. By carefully examining and probing Job's life, one can draw the following observations about his downward spiral into depression.

1. Job's depression was directly related to the circumstances he had faced. Christians are not machines who have no feelings. Having a loved one die or going through a difficult financial reversal are legitimate reasons for being depressed. Some Christians erroneously believe they are supposed to live life so perfectly that no circumstances affect them. All humans are emotional creatures who are very much affected by the circumstances they must endure. The incredible pain of losing a child brings incredible heartache; that loss often brings incredible depression. Likewise, intense, indescribable loneliness comes with losing a spouse. A huge vacancy comes in life with the death of a spouse.

I believe I can empathize with people who suffer with difficult diseases. My mother was diagnosed with two very difficult diseases, and my dad spent an entire year traveling and trying to find help for my mother. Finally, he found a doctor who had some answers and was giving them a little hope. I watched my parents endure this time of searching for help. I also watched them endure the thoughtless comments of others. We were sitting in a restaurant when someone said to my mother, "We have been thinking about you and praying for you. I believe I know what your problem is, Marlene. If you'll just get right with God, all your problems will go away."

I still remember the pain and emotion that imprudent remark brought to me. How much more it must have knifed through my mother who was suffering with a terrible disease. A person can be right with God and be suffering. A person can be right with God and be very depressed at the same time.

2. Job's terrible circumstances were not brought on by his living too badly, but by living too good. Some casually remark, "So-and-so is depressed; he must be living wrong." Job was the best Christian in the world; he was a perfect and upright man who hated evil. How could Job be the best Christian in the world and be depressed? Job's depression was not the result of living a sinful life; on the contrary, he was living righteously. Depression attacks everyone—from the weakest Christian who hasn't read his Bible, hasn't been on schedule, doesn't go soul winning, and barely attends church to the godliest person on the face of the earth.

3. The best Christian of that day also suffered the deepest depression of his day. Some of the greatest names in Christianity, including Martin Luther and Charles Spurgeon, lived very mercurial, up-and-down lives. They tried everything known in their time to combat depression. Some of the prophets listed in the Bible were very depressed men at times.

One's depression may be the result of being a very good Christian, or it may be the result of being a very undisciplined Christian. Therefore, it would behoove all of us to refrain from judging anyone while he or she is suffering with depression.

4. Job's depression was related to his intense emotional nature. Job was an emotionally passionate man who obviously feared God. He eschewed evil, which means he spat it out and despised it. He loved God with all of his heart, and he hated sin with all of his heart. One reason why Job suffered in depression so acutely was that his intense ability to feel so deeply afforded depression a great haven.

Depression comes to some because they have a greater capacity for highs, and that also brings a greater capacity for lows. A positive person can be so negative because he is so positive! The man who soars high above the clouds with God can also be deeply depressed!

Depression reminds me of a huge hill just south of town where my friends and I loved to ride our bicycles. A little creek cut through the middle of that steep hill. We had great fun riding to the top of one hill, pedaling as fast as we could down the hill, coasting across the creek and up the other side until our momentum ended, and we would then begin pedaling once again to reach the top of the second hill. The faster we rode down the first hill, the higher our momentum carried us up the second hill. Woe be to any of us who stopped for a pit stop at the creek! We would have to say "goodbye" to pedaling up the second hill. We had to get off the bike and push it to the top of the hill.

God works in cycles. Going down to go higher is scriptural. Though our Lord Jesus Christ was rich, for our sakes He became poor that through His poverty we might be made rich. Those who soar the highest with God also experience the greatest lows with God.

Job's depression was indirectly caused by a dispute between God and Satan; however, Job never learned that fact. No one really knows why depression or negative circumstances come. Perhaps God and the Devil have discussed you, and God believes He can trust you like He trusted Job. When the Devil was given liberty to take Job's health and Job passed the test, the Devil had nothing further to say. The debate had silenced Satan. Quite possibly the person who is presently experiencing deep depression is giving God incredible ammunition to use against the Devil. Your life has been judged worthy for God to mention your name to Satan.

How Did Job Finally Get Out of Depression?

1. Job's friends did not bring him out of his depression. Job's three best friends took seven days off from work to do nothing but comfort Job. However, they were so stunned by his excruciating pain that they never offered one word of consolation. His friends surely tried because much of the book of Job is a discussion between Job and his friends. Seeking friends is not the answer for depression.

2. Job's circumstances did not change first. Some think erroneously, "If I can just hold on until my situation changes...." What if your circumstances don't change? What if your health does not improve? What if your financial condition does not change? Job had no change in his circumstances until after the depression.

3. Job's health did not improve. He was sick until God ended his captivity. Job was miserable in his disease, but he lived with that condition until after the depression lifted.

4. No medicine lifted Job's spirit. No mention of medicine's being prescribed is found in the book of Job. No Prozac for depression or morphine for the pain was offered.

5. Job's depression was lifted when he prayed for his friends. *"And the LORD turned the captivity of Job, when he prayed for his friends."* (Job 42:10a) Every prayer that Job cried out from chapter 2 through chapter 42 was the same prayer: "Deliver me!" Finally in chapter 42, he focused on his three friends and prayed for them. When Job asked God to take care of his friends, God delivered Job from his captivity and lifted his spirit.

As long as the depressed person is looking to God to deliver him and as long as he is looking for an excuse for his depression, or trying to analyze it, or seeking medical help for it, he will remain depressed. Depression ends when a person starts living for others. The Lord turned Job's captivity when he prayed for his friends. The simplest of truth works!

The number one reason why a person gets depressed is that the tension is turned on, and the number one reason why he stays depressed is that he keeps focusing on how to get out of his depression. The quickest cure for depression is to stop worrying about how to get out of it; start helping someone else get out of theirs! "Others, Lord, yes, others, Let this my motto be. / Help me to live for others, That I may live like Thee"—depression free!

CHAPTER THIRTEEN

THE FORMULA FOR DEPRESSION

"Blessed be the God and Father of our Lord Jesus Christ, which according to his abundant mercy hath begotten us again unto a lively hope by the resurrection of Jesus Christ from the dead, To an inheritance incorruptible, and undefiled, and that fadeth not away, reserved in heaven for you, Who are kept by the power of God through faith unto salvation ready to be revealed in the last time. Wherein ye greatly rejoice, though now for a season, if need be, ye are in heaviness through manifold temptations: That the trial of your faith, being much more precious than of gold that perisheth, though it be tried with fire, might be found unto praise and honour and glory at the appearing of Jesus Christ: Whom having not seen, ye love; in whom, though now ye see him not, yet believing, ye rejoice with joy unspeakable and full of glory: Receiving the end of your faith, even the salvation of your souls." (I Peter 1:3-9)

As we have already established, the Bible word *heaviness* is synonymous with the modern word "depression." *Heaviness* means "to despair." Obviously, God does not want a Christian to live a life of depression.

Through the years, I have heard the following formula for depression:

Insult + Anger x Self-pity = Depression

This formula describes how and why a person becomes depressed. This formula for depression can be applied to anyone. Elijah fled when Jezebel threatened to kill him (insult). He became upset at God because God did not deliver him from Jezebel (anger). Elijah ended up in a cave bemoaning his sad situation (self-pity). Just days before, he had called down fire from Heaven.

Job, who was the best Christian of his day, became depressed. From Job's life we established the fact that being a good Christian does not prevent one from falling susceptible to depression. "*Wherein ye greatly rejoice, though now for a season, if need be, ye are in heaviness* [depression] *through manifold temptations* [testing or proving]: *That the trial of your faith, being much more precious than of gold....*" (I Peter 1:6, 7) This Scripture passage is addressing believers who are depressed.

The factors that bring or cause depression are usually out of a person's control. However, understanding and using this truth can help a person control his depression. He can have control over the severity of his depression and the length of his depression. Allowing depression to take such a hold that a Christian despairs of his very life should be very rare.

It is a common mistake among many Christians to think that salvation brings freedom from serious problems. On the contrary, Christians are not problem free; in fact, Christians may quite possibly have more problems because they pose a threat to the kingdom of darkness. Christians already have the normal stress of meeting financial obligations, building a strong marriage, rearing children, and confronting a myriad of problems that occur in the routines of life. The Devil is never happy when a person gets saved; he delights in bringing "speed bumps" to add more problems to a Christian. Though Christians suffer more problems and are not problem free, they also have better solutions. The saved person has far more powerful weaponry in his arsenal to fight depression.

The formula for depression, Insult + Anger x Self-pity = Depression, is the same for the Christian as well as the non-Christian.

1. All depression begins with a root cause. That root cause is a disturbance in life which creates either physical injury or emotional insult. Most of these major root causes or insults fit within the following categories:

A. Disappointment. Great disappointment brings anger about a situation often considered unfair. Being laid off at work, receiving a bad medical report, or being overlooked for a promotion are kinds of disappointments that come into a person's life that can bring anger. The list is endless.

B. Low self-esteem. A person with a low self-esteem is usually a perfectionist who sets an unrealistic goal for himself and then fails to reach his own goal. Generally, a perfectionist is too hard on himself and cannot accept the fact that he will never be perfect. Christians should surely strive for perfection—within reason. I believe that improvement is a much better goal than perfection.

C. Unfair comparisons. It is good to have role models; in fact, every person needs role models. Ladies who are trying to rear sons alone should point their boys toward some male role models. A role model is not someone who brings depression to a person's life; rather, the role model is supposed to inspire one to achieve loftier goals. II Corinthians 10:12 says, "...*but they measuring themselves by themselves, and comparing themselves among themselves, are not wise.*" According to the Bible, it is not wise to say, "I wish I was like So-and-so." The sooner a person accepts that fact, the less prone he will be to depression.

D. Feeling trapped in an impossible situation. This desperate feeling is the catalyst, or the spark plug, for depression. Feeling imprisoned in an unhappy, hopeless marriage; feeling locked and paralyzed in a wheelchair; or being caught in the grip of postpartum blues brings on deep depression. People who live with these kinds of difficulties often live in depression.

E. A disorganized mind or schedule. Organize your life and have a plan. If you do not structure your life, you are a candidate for depression. Maybe all you need to do is buy a schedule book or calendar and write down what you need to do. Get your mind organized and get your schedule organized. Brother Hyles often said, "Let your schedule be your boss." An organized schedule will help keep one from being depressed.

F. Rejection. An intensive study of the school shootings found one common denominator—everyone who pulled a trigger and killed others had been bullied and rejected by his peers. Rejection is an insult that wraps tentacles around a person's heart and eventually chokes out the good.

G. Inadequate goals. Never stop working and never stop having a plan. Keep a purpose in life because those who live a life of idleness with no plans are great candidates for depression.

2. The natural and non-Christian reaction to an insult is

anger. Anger is a microscopic inspection of one's problem. The formula says, "Insult + Anger." When a person's security has been threatened, his sense of pride responds with a self-protective attitude and a self-righteous anger that declares, "That's not fair!" Saying that a life in a wheelchair is not fair is to remove Romans 8:28 from the Bible. *"And we know that all things work together for good to them that love God, to them who are the called according to his purpose."* To take Romans 8:28 from the Bible leaves only human reasoning that cultivates anger.

James 1:20 says, *"For the wrath of man worketh not the righteousness of God."* Self-righteous anger brings unrighteous attitudes. A person's emotions become supercharged with the feeling of injustice, and "road rage" results. An unassuming postal worker walks into the post office and kills seven employees, or a "good" boy murders 15 of his friends. The insult may very well be out of a person's hands to control, but the anger is his to control. Whether or not he allows his anger to take control is his decision.

Anger is a reaction, not the action. The action comes out of an insult. An insult comes from an unexpected source, and it wounds you. The next response of anger is your choice. You did not have a decision to make when the action occurred, but you do have a decision whether to be angry about it.

3.   **Anger is the fastest way to short-circuit the power and influence of the Holy Spirit within you.** If you want to lose the power of the Holy Spirit to help you, to protect you, and to guard you, then get angry and stay angry. Ephesians 4:30 says, *"And grieve not the Holy Spirit of God...."* Anger is the leading cause of grieving the Holy Spirit. Colossians 3:8 says, *"But now ye also put off all these; anger, wrath, malice...."* Proverbs 22:24 says, *"Make no friendship with an angry man; and with a furious man thou shalt*

not go." The Holy Spirit, the Comforter, does not abide in an angry person. That is why anger makes a Christian act like an out-of-control, unsaved person.

How to Conquer Anger

The injustices that come into our lives cannot humanly be prevented. Diagnoses of cancer will come. A company will go bankrupt, leaving people without employment. We cannot stop the injury from coming, but we can stop the anger from building and ultimately bringing depression. The ball is in our court; we must stop the anger from taking root.

1. Put it off. As we walk through life and get insulted, our first reaction is anger. Resist the anger; it's not the correct reaction! Stop, back up, and wait.

2. Use soft words. *"A soft answer turneth away wrath: but grievous words stir up anger."* (Proverbs 15:1) A soft answer is always the proper response to an injury.

3. Count your blessings. An attitude of gratitude is the best way to derail anger. When the insult comes, remember all the good...church, Bible, salvation, a good spouse, happy children, gainful employment, Heaven! Counting our blessings derails and defuses anger!

4. Express your love. I Peter 4:8 says, *"And above all things have fervent charity among yourselves...."* Charity is not love that is felt; rather, charity is love that is expressed. A charitable person gives to those who do not deserve the charity. Proverbs 21:14 says, *"A gift in secret pacifieth anger: and a reward in the bosom strong wrath."* The best thing to do when an insult comes is back off, stand down, speak soft words, count your blessings, and give a gift to someone who doesn't deserve the gift. That gift in secret pacifies the anger of the one who gave!

Give in secret. Quietly express your love behind the scenes. Do something nice anonymously.

5. Hospitality. "To run to the aid of someone" is the meaning of the word *hospitality*. Hospitality comes from the root word *hospital*. Rush to the aid of the weak and the downhearted ones. Whereas anger is the microscopic inspection of one thing that bothers you, hospitality is getting focused on someone who desperately needs you.

To be sure, there are no quick fixes in the Christian life. We live in a world of angry people—even Christians—who are wreaking havoc in their homes, in their marriages, in the lives of their children, and in their workplaces. Appropriating the Holy Spirit's help in utilizing this formula to combat insult and anger is the key to conquering depression in a Christian's arsenal. The next part of the formula, self-pity, will be addressed in the next chapter.

CHAPTER FOURTEEN

"YOU FORGOT SOMETHING, ELIJAH!"

"And Ahab told Jezebel all that Elijah had done, and withal how he had slain all the prophets with the sword. Then Jezebel sent a messenger unto Elijah, saying, So let the gods do to me, and more also, if I make not thy life as the life of one of them by to morrow about this time. And when he saw that, he arose, and went for his life, and came to Beer-sheba, which belongeth to Judah, and left his servant there. But he himself went a day's journey into the wilderness, and came and sat down under a juniper tree: and he requested for himself that he might die; and said, It is enough; now, O LORD, take away my life; for I am not better than my fathers. And as he lay and slept under a juniper tree, behold, then an angel touched him, and said unto him, Arise and eat. And he looked, and, behold, there was a cake baken on the coals, and a cruse of water at his head. And he did eat and drink, and laid him down again. And the angel of the LORD came again the second time, and touched him, and said, Arise and eat; because the journey is too great for thee. And he arose, and did eat and drink, and went in the strength of that meat forty days and forty nights unto Horeb the mount of God. And he came thither unto a cave, and lodged there; and, behold, the word of the LORD came to *him, and he said unto him, What doest thou here, Elijah?"* (I Kings 19:1-9)

THE STORY OF ELIJAH in I Kings 19 is an intimate look at a very depressed man of God. From his story can be drawn the absolute basic cause of all depression. To be sure, several common causes are the catalyst to bring on depression—physical difficulties, disappointment, low self-esteem, unfair comparisons, sickness and disease, feeling trapped in an intolerable situation, postpartum blues, a disorganized mind, a disorganized schedule, rejection of others, or inadequate goals, to name a few. Many of these catalysts apply to Elijah.

Elijah had just experienced a mighty victory on Mt. Carmel over the 850 false prophets of Baal. He called down fire from Heaven and killed them all. An enraged Jezebel sent word that his life was forfeit. *"Then Jezebel sent a messenger unto Elijah, saying, So let the gods do to me, and more also, if I make not thy life as the life of one of them by to morrow about this time."* (I Kings 19:2) Obviously, Ahab and Jezebel were not pleased with Elijah's slaughter of their prophets. Rejection is a common cause of depression, and Elijah was rejected by the highest authority in the land. That would be comparable to the President of the United States letting you know that he did not appreciate you. When the world makes fun of people, this rejection gives way to hurt feelings.

When properly dressed, young ladies face the jeers of the worldly girls; I always wonder why they would care or worry about their rejection. Unfortunately though, we do feel rejected, and that rejection can even lead to a depression about being a Christian.

I Kings 19:4, *"But he himself went a day's journey into the wilderness, and came and sat down under a juniper tree: and he requested for himself that he might die; and said, It is enough; now, O Lord, take away my life; for I am not better than my fathers."* I could get depressed if I compared myself to my predecessor. A little lea-guer cannot compare himself to Babe Ruth or Mickey Mantle. The Bible stresses the fact that we are not supposed to measure ourselves by others. II Corinthians 10:12 says, *"...they measuring themselves by themselves, and comparing themselves among them-selves, are not wise."*

Elijah was excusing his depression by saying that he had not yet reached the level of his father. Elijah had called down fire from Heaven, slew 850 false prophets, and was bemoaning the fact that he was not as good as his father or father-in-law or grandfather was!

"And he arose, and did eat and drink, and went in the strength of that meat forty days and forty nights unto Horeb the mount of God." (I Kings 19:8) Elijah ate two meals and went forty days and forty nights on those two meals. That lack of sustenance would cause anyone to feel weak and very exhausted.

"And the hand of the LORD was on Elijah; and he girded up his loins, and ran before Ahab to the entrance of Jezreel." (I Kings 18:46) In this incredible account, Elijah outran a chariot drawn by two horses for 30 miles. In other words, he ran a longer dis-tance than today's marathons, which are 26 miles and a few hun-dred yards. Elijah was desperately in need of a good meal, a good night's rest, and some recovery time.

The bottom line is that Elijah had all the common reasons why people become depressed, and humanly speaking, he had a right to feel somewhat depressed. Some of the best Christians in the world are susceptible to depression. However, the main rea-son for Elijah's depression was not due to fatigue, or exhaustion, or sleep depravation, or lack of sustenance. Rather, the greatest source of depression and despair in Elijah's life is found in I Kings 19:10, 14, *"And he said, I have been very jealous for the LORD God of hosts: for the children of Israel have forsaken thy covenant, thrown down thine altars, and slain thy prophets with the sword; and I, even I only, am left; and they seek my life, to take it away....And he said, I have been very jealous for the LORD God of hosts: because the children of Israel have forsaken thy covenant, thrown down thine altars, and slain thy prophets with sword; and I, even I only, am left; and they seek my life, to take it away."* The source of the depression and despair of Elijah can be summed up in one word—self-pity. We blame everything for our depression—exhaustion, the postpartum blues, a chemical imbalance, the wrong diet, hypoglycemia, loss, tragedy, grief, injury, and hurt—to name a few of the common excuses. But the bottom line reason for everyone who feels like life is not worth living is self-pity.

Depressed people despise that analysis! However, the only pathway out of depression and despair is to face the ugly monster that drags a person into the slough of despondency and that monster is self-pity. Every person who indulges in self-pity will eventually end up in the quagmire of depression and despair. The bottom line reason for giving way to depression is the excuse that Elijah gave: "**I** am the only one left"; he fell prey to self-pity. Elijah wasn't the only prophet standing against Ahab and Jezebel; God told him that 7,000 other prophets had not bowed down to Baal.

Psalm 69:20, *"Reproach hath broken my heart; and I am full of heaviness: and I looked for some to take pity, but there was none; and for comforters, but I found none."* The reason why David received no comfort was that he had so much self-pity. Depressed people sustain a wound, nurse that wound, and justify their anger and their hurt until they have swallowed themselves with feeling sorry for themselves; self-pity becomes their life.

1. Self-pity looks at what it cannot do, not what it can do. Self-pity says, "Do you see what I lost?" Self-pity stays focused on what is unfixable, irretrievable, broken beyond repair, unrecoverable, broken without remedy, and gone forever. Instead of living in the land of regret over what is gone, look instead at what you do have!

An 18 year old who was driving his motorcycle through San Francisco at 5:00 a.m. was struck by a milk truck making deliveries. The gas tank on the motorcycle ruptured, exploded into flames, and the young man was burned over 95 percent of his body. After enduring horrific pain, skin grafts, and disfigurement, he moved to Colorado, went into business, and became quite wealthy. When his own airplane crashed, his spine was broken, resulting in paralysis from the waist down. Though burned and scarred over 95 percent of his body, paralyzed from the waist down, and confined to a wheelchair, this man became the state senator of Colorado.

While he was campaigning for office, a member of the press said, "You have been burned horribly, have extensive disfigurement, and are paralyzed from the waist down. You have lost so much of what life is. How can you keep such optimism to think you are worthy of running for the Senate?"

This candidate had an astonishing answer! "Before I was injured in those two crashes, I probably could have done 10,000 things in life. Now I can only do 9,000 things in life. Shall I despair over the 1,000 that I cannot do, or shall I pursue the 9,000 that I can?"

That man's attitude is the answer to depression. A person cannot live life looking at what he lost; he must look at all there is to gain! Self-pity looks at what it cannot do, not at what it can do. We still have something in life that is worthy of living, worthy of pursuing.

2. Self-pity is the love of self more than the love of others. I read the story of a pilot who was shot down in Vietnam and listed as missing in action. For four years his wife lived with conflicting thoughts and emotions of, "Is he alive? Is he dead?" She had three little boys to rear who had barely known their father; she was desperately trying to be both a mother and a father to them. She became so severely depressed that she quit eating and lost weight until she was down to 89 pounds.

She was taken to a counselor, and he listened to her whole story. She shared how she could not deal with the uncertainty and would rather know that he was dead than to live life with all of the uncertainty.

This counselor said that he had never wanted to weep so much for someone who had such a human reason to be depressed; but when she made that statement, he told her that the reason for her depression was her self-pity. He further explained that she was feeling so sorry for herself that she couldn't see that she was dwelling in self-pity. "You love yourself more than you love your husband," he ended.

When she denied his diagnosis, he asked, "Then why would you rather have your husband dead so you can feel better? While there is hope that he might be alive, wouldn't you want to thank God that he is not dead?"

For four years this wife ignored her three children because she didn't know what was happening to her husband. Suddenly it occurred to her that she had three boys to rear. The lady said, "I never saw it like that before."

The depressed person wants his security blanket. He wants

that feeling that he is in control of his life. Self-pity is wanting your world back in control instead of loving others. Self-pity is the love of self more than a love for anyone else. Take yourself out of the center of your universe.

3. Self-pity is not changed by a change in circumstances. One of the biggest lies of Satan involves divorce. The Devil alleges that divorcing and remarrying will bring about a change of circumstances thereby bringing happiness. A person can get divorced and remarried until he holds the world record and is listed in the *Guinness Book of World Records*; he probably will not find the happiness he is seeking by changing his circumstances. Paying alimony and child support to previous spouses will surely change a person's circumstances—but certainly not in a positive way! The only way to endure difficult circumstances is by appropriating the grace of God.

4. Self-pity is a contradiction of Romans 8:28. *"And we know that all things work together for good to them that love God, to them who are the called according to his purpose."* If Romans 8:28 is wrong, then the entire Bible is foolishness, God isn't alive, and Christians are wasting their valuable time living their lives for a lie. However, Romans 8:28 is true, and the person who believes otherwise is full of self-pity. Self-pity contradicts Romans 8:28. Self-pity looks at what it cannot do instead of what it can do. Self-pity is the love of self greater than a love of others. Self-pity is not changed by a person's circumstances.

5. Self-pity is a rejection of God's grace. Self-pity says that God is not big enough to give anyone grace sufficient enough for the problems he is facing. We reject grace by saying that it is not sufficient. Even the Apostle Paul doubted the sufficiency of God's grace. Let His grace cover you, and humble yourself, and say, "God, You are big enough for my problem."

The Cure for Self-Pity

A. Faith. I Peter 1:6, 7a, *"Wherein ye greatly rejoice, though now for a season, if need be, ye are in heaviness* [depression] *through manifold temptations* [testing]: *That the trial of your faith…."* Testing and problems and injuries and loss and grief and pain and rejection and sickness and disease are tests of every person's faith. All we need is a Christ Who hung on a cross, Who was buried, and Who rose again from the dead. Every problem we face is a test of the faith we have in the God Who is available to help us pass the test.

B. Grace. Is God big enough to give the Christian enough grace? Grace is that internal desire and the spiritual willpower that enables every person to face the trials of life with joy in his heart and a smile on his lips, even though there is a tear in his eye and a quiver in his voice. Paul opened nine epistles with the words, *"Grace be unto you."* He was saying that whatever comes in life, we can handle it. Grace has a tear streaming down its face and says, "God is able." The grace of God was great enough to cancel out and forgive every sin on our record, and the grace of God is big enough to handle any trial of our faith.

Faith and grace are formidable weapons to use against self-pity; however, the most powerful weapon in the Christian's arsenal against self-pity is **thanksgiving**. Self-pity and thanksgiving cannot co-habit. Self-pity devours and swallows up gratitude; thanksgiving pushes out self-pity.

Remember Elijah on Mt. Carmel? An altar was built, a trench was dug around the altar, the trench was filled with water, and the altar was baptized with water. After all the preparations were made, then Elijah called down fire from Heaven. Not only was the wood on the altar burned, the stones were also consumed! Elijah was the only man in the Bible to call down fire from Heaven, but not once in this account did Elijah ever look to Heaven and say, "Thank You, God!"

If you are depressed, you have lost your thankfulness. How can a person be thankful for what he has to face? I Thessalonians 5:18 says, "**In** *every thing give thanks....*" The Bible does not say, "**For** every thing give thanks." This principle is well illustrated by the three Hebrew boys, Shadrach, Meshach, and Abed-nego, who were bound and thrown into the fiery furnace. At Nebuchadnezzar's command, the furnace was heated seven times hotter—so hot that their executioners were devoured by the heat. When King Nebuchadnezzar looked into the furnace, he was astonished: *"...Did not we cast three men bound into the midst of the fire?...Lo, I see four men loose, walking in the midst of the fire, and they have no hurt; and the form of the fourth is like the Son of God."* (Daniel 3:24, 25) Do you honestly think Shadrach was thankful **for** the fiery furnace? Of course not! He was thankful **in** the fiery furnace because he was sustained in the presence of the Son of the living God. The deeper our problems, the more severe our calamity and injury, the more present our God is for us—*"...a very present help in trouble."* (Psalm 46:1)

Self-pity, the love of self, contradicts Romans 8:28. It contradicts and rejects the grace of God. The only way for us to conquer self-pity is by recognizing that troubles are a test of faith. God has sufficient grace, and we must give thanks for the testing of our faith. Giving thanks will devour self-pity. The test may bring sadness or pain or disappointment, but if we give thanks, we won't be like Elijah under the juniper tree!

CHAPTER FIFTEEN

PROTECTING MYSELF
FROM DEPRESSION

"Again there was a day when the sons of God came to present themselves before the LORD, and Satan came also among them to present himself before the LORD. And the LORD said unto Satan, From whence comest thou? And Satan answered the LORD, and said, From going to and fro in the earth, and from walking up and down in it. And the LORD said unto Satan, Hast thou considered my servant Job, that there is none like him in the earth, a perfect and an upright man, one that feareth God, and escheweth evil? and still he holdeth fast his integrity, although thou movedst me against him, to destroy him without cause. And Satan answered the LORD, and said, Skin for skin, yea, all that a man hath will he give for his life. But put forth thine hand now, and touch his bone and his flesh, and he will curse thee to thy face. And the LORD said unto Satan, Behold, he is in thine hand; but save his life. So went Satan forth from the presence of the LORD, and smote Job with sore boils from the sole of his foot unto his crown. And he took him a potsherd to scrape himself withal; and he sat down among the ashes. Then said his wife unto him, Dost thou still retain thine integrity? curse God, and die. But he said unto her, Thou speakest as one of the foolish women speaketh. What? shall we

*receive good at the hand of God, and shall we not receive evil? In all
this did not Job sin with his lips."* (Job 2:1-10)

As WE HAVE ALREADY established, an accurate formula
for depression is "Injury + Anger x Self-pity = Depression."
Self-pity is that root cause of all depression because it is the "I-
feel-sorry-for-myself" syndrome. Once the self-pity stage of the
formula is reached, the person will become thoroughly
depressed. He will not get out of his depression until he realizes
that he has bathed his wound in self-pity, and the only way to
counteract feeling sorry for himself is through thanksgiving.
Gratitude and self-pity cannot cohabit the same dwelling place.
No one can simultaneously have a thankful heart and feel self-
pity. A person full of self-pity might express some words of
thanksgiving, but he will not feel thankful. The cure for self-pity
is gratitude.

The first ingredient in the formula, "injury," bears a closer
look. We have previously established that injury is that external
enemy that disrupts a person's security. Anything that upsets the
rhythm and cadence in a person's life is an injury. It is the insult
that invades the spirit and causes the heart to be grieved. Injury
in and of itself is not depression. Injuries are the negative circumstances of life that come into every person's life.

If the person can work through his injury, he will have no
reason to become angry. If he does not embrace anger, he will not
eventually feel sorry for himself. If he does not feel sorry for himself, he will not become depressed. Life's injuries are different;
what comes into the life of one person doesn't always enter the
life of another. An injury might be a chronic disease, disappointment, rejection, fatigue, or feeling trapped in an intolerable situ-

ation. The injury factor is the key to all depression.

God provides a way every person can protect himself from depression. No one really wants to dwell in the neighborhood of depression. Unfortunately, some who are swallowed by their depression remain at that somewhat comfortable habitat because the effort to leave takes greater energy than the energy behind the circumstances that put them there.

Injury comes from two sources: God-inflicted injury and self-inflicted injury. God-inflicted injuries involved those events which cannot be humanly controlled. Job downsizing, the death of a loved one, or medical issues are just a few of the issues that cannot be humanly controlled. Neither can we control the testing and temptations that come as I Peter 1:6 says, *"Wherein ye greatly rejoice, though now for a season, if need be, ye are in heaviness through manifold temptations."* Testing comes our way via Satanic persecution, demonic oppression, and the external circumstances in which we didn't have a vote. These are also God-inflicted injuries because God allows them.

Self-inflicted injuries are the most common cause of depression. Often they are the result of ignorance or disobedience or because of bad company or a bad environment or a bad schedule.

In many cases of depression, the injury begins as an act of God. Even though Elijah had called down fire from Heaven and had rid the land of 850 false prophets of Baal, he became thoroughly depressed. Elijah's God-inflicted injury was the message of rejection by Ahab and Jezebel. To be sure, Elijah had no control over Ahab and Jezebel's reaction, and he could not understand why they wanted him dead. His initial injury allowed by God eventually brought depression and despair.

Elijah could have said, "I have no control over Ahab and

Jezebel," and accepted his God-inflicted injury; however, he compounded it with a self-inflicted injury. He ran a distance of 30 miles faster than a horse could run, went one day's journey into the wilderness, and then traveled 150 miles—on only two meals. His self-inflicted injury was traveling 180 miles on two meals and very little sleep. Bad schedule and poor dietary habits can lead to depression. Elijah no longer wanted to live because of the self-inflicted injury added to the God-inflicted injury. He had no control over the God-inflicted injuries that came his way, but he could have controlled the self-inflicted injuries that compounded the problem and brought the anger and the self-pity which caused the depression.

Circumstances beyond a person's control must be received with faith and praise. Faith and praise are like two receivers in a football game. We have to receive the circumstances of God like a football receiver receives the punted football. When God sends a circumstance our way, we can't bat it away; we have to receive it, and our receivers are called faith and praise.

The time between the injury and the praise is the measure of a person's spiritual maturity. Eventually everyone does give praise for the injury. The key is to instantly let faith and praise rejoice in the injury. When Job's injuries came, his automatic reflex action was to receive the injury with an incredible maturity. Job 1:20, 21 says, "*Then Job arose, and rent his mantle, and shaved his head, and fell down upon the ground, and worshipped, And said, Naked came I out of my mother's womb, and naked shall I return thither: the LORD gave, and the LORD hath taken away; blessed be the name of the LORD.*" This passage reveals the proper reaction and response to every God-inflicted injury. Job said, "*...blessed be the name of the LORD.*" The one who cannot say "blessed be the name of the Lord" in the injuries has not earned the right to say "blessed be the name of the Lord" in the good times. One is not a spiritual Christian to the degree that he praises God for the good times; he is a spiritual Christian to the degree that his praise response time to an injury is extremely brief.

In Job 2:9, 10, "*Then said his wife unto him, Dost thou still retain thine integrity? curse God, and die. But he said unto her, Thou speakest as one of the foolish women speaketh. What? shall we receive good at the hand of God, and shall we not receive evil? In all this did not Job sin with his lips.*" At this point in Job's life, he had lost everything, including his health. He said to his wife, "You didn't mind receiving the good things from God. If you are able to receive the good things from God, you must learn how to receive the bad things from God." Mrs. Job wanted to be a receiver of only the good.

Paul said "*...I have learned, in whatsoever state I am, therewith to be content. I know both how to be abased, and I know how to abound....*" (Philippians 4:11, 12) Paul understood both sides of the equation. He was a receiver of good and a receiver of ill, but his response was the same—"Blessed be the name of the Lord!" It is not enough for a person to enjoy the goodness of the Lord; he must also enjoy the Lord in the bad times.

Have you learned to receive the God-inflicted injury? Consider the following thoughts about receiving an injury that comes via the hands of a loving God.

1. Circumstances beyond my control must be received with praise and faith. I am a strong "sovereignist," one who believes that God is in control. I believe with all my heart that God is on a throne in Heaven, and I believe what He said in Daniel 4:17, "*...the most High ruleth in the kingdom of men, and giveth it to whomsoever he will, and setteth up over it the basest of* men." God put Fidel Castro in Cuba. He put Bill Clinton and George W. Bush in the White House. God also allows cancer to come to the life of a loved one. God allows people to die. Nothing happens to anyone without God's personal approval.

My faith tells me that nothing comes to me without being personally approved by my loving Heavenly Father. My faith will not allow me to override the mind of God. My faith is like a shock absorber. When a devastating injury comes to me, I receive it, and even if I do not like it, my faith steps in and says, "That is not for me to question."

A person's faith is the Supreme Court of justice in his spirit. When the lesser courts of human reasoning and human suffering judge a circumstance to be unfair, the case is automatically retried in the courtroom of faith, and God is always declared righteous. Whatever the injury is, human reasoning often steps in and says, "I don't think it is fair or just. Why would a loving Heavenly Father let that happen?" As soon as human reasoning judges an injury to be unfair, unwanted, unjustified, unkind, unnecessary, and unneeded, the case immediately proceeds to the appellate court system all the way to the courtroom of faith—the Supreme Court. Any lesser court ruling is automatically overruled.

Faith listens carefully to the case. Human reasoning argues the case like a powerful attorney, but faith declares that God is not on trial. Human reasoning must bow to the Supreme Court of faith and concede. Faith is the courtroom that always automatically declares God as righteous and just.

As soon as faith makes its ruling, praise follows: "Blessed be the name of the Lord!" Job did not get depressed until his three human-reasoning friends came to tell him what was wrong. Nothing in Job's reaction until that time was remotely close to depression. God inflicted injury, and Job sinned not. He was not at the point of despair until his three friends opened their mouths and tried to offer plausible explanations for his heartaches and distresses. No doubt Job's friends meant well and were sincere, but they were the catalyst to his depression.

What is praise? Praise is recognizing and honoring God for Who He is. Praise is different from thanksgiving which honors His deeds that He does for us. Praise honors His character for Who He is. For instance, thanksgiving is a wife thanking her husband for the roses and other thoughtful gifts she received on Valentine's Day. Praise is saying, "I feel so secure when I am around you." Praise is a wife's thanking her husband for his strength, his wisdom, his masculinity, his wisdom, and his char- acter. Praising God is thanking Him for His unchangeableness, His immutability, His eternal Word, His mercy, His love, and His understanding. When praise follows faith, depression cannot penetrate.

When injury comes, start praising, "Blessed be the name of the Lord." Depression is not welcome in the life of a Christian who praises. Depression cannot cohabit with a man whose faith says, "The Lord gave; blessed be the name of the Lord. The Lord has taken away; blessed be the name of the Lord."

When I was a Sunday school bus captain of a route in East Chicago, I invited a mother to ride the bus with her children. When she refused, I asked her why she would not come with her children. She told me that she did not believe in God because He allowed her mother be murdered.

"God knows how you feel more than anyone else does," I offered. "I'm sure your mother was unjustly murdered, but the Son of God was also unjustly murdered. God knows what it is like to have a family member murdered. Don't blame God for the unrighteous deeds of some wicked people."

She asked, "If your God is so big, then why didn't your God stop it?"

"For the same reason He didn't stop six million Jews from being murdered in World War II," I explained. "For the same reason He didn't stop the Somalis from dying of starvation. For the same reason, some heathen tribes are still cannibals. Many wicked things happen now, but it all started because of sin. Your anger against God is a testimony to the sin in your heart."

Our conversation continued until she finally declared, "I am not going to have God."

"Listen very carefully," I warned her. "If you don't get over this bitterness in your heart about God's letting your mother be murdered, you are going to reap it in your kids."

Ten years later I saw that woman, and I asked, "Do you remember our conversation?"

"I remember well what you told me," she admitted. "My daughters have followed me. They don't go to church or Sunday school, and they hate God. Why did that happen?"

"The same reason I told you ten years ago," I said. "Bad things happen to good people, and when you don't handle it properly, you become angry, filled with self-pity, and depressed."

Both faith and praise are pieces of armor God has given every Christian to use against depression. Faith is having the same reaction toward the bad as one does toward the good. Faith is saying that God is always righteous. Faith is accepting the good and the bad. Praise is thanking God for being strong, for being on His throne, for being in charge, and for being longsuffering. Faith is a choice. Praise is a choice. Just like every great spiritual decision, having faith and praising God are choices.

CHAPTER SIXTEEN

SELF-INFLICTED DEPRESSION

"Then Jonah prayed unto the LORD his God out of the fish's belly, And said, I cried by reason of mine affliction unto the LORD, and he heard me; out of the belly of hell cried I, and thou heardest my voice. For thou hadst cast me into the deep, in the midst of the seas; and the floods compassed me about: all thy billows and thy waves passed over me. Then I said, I am cast out of thy sight; yet I will look again toward thy holy temple. The waters compassed me about, even to the soul: the depth closed me round about, the weeds were wrapped about my head. I went down to the bottoms of the mountains; the earth with her bars was about me for ever: yet hast thou brought up my life from corruption, O LORD my God. When my soul fainted within me, I remembered the LORD: and my prayer came in unto thee, into thine holy temple. They that observe lying vanities forsake their own mercy. But I will sacrifice unto thee with the voice of thanksgiving; I will pay that that I have vowed. Salvation is of the LORD. And the LORD spake unto the fish, and it vomited out Jonah upon the dry land." (Jonah 2)

SELF-INFLICTED INJURIES ARE the most common cause of depression; that is, we bring it on ourselves. All depression begins with an insult or an injury—a disappointment, discouragement, postpartum blues, an illness, a financial reversal, the collapse of a relationship, harsh words, or an injury to a loved one. Somehow a person is knocked off track by a personal injury.

Within a brief time frame, Job suffered the loss of his children, his health, his wealth, his employees, his businesses, and the respect of his wife. Elijah, the prophet, was devastated by a death warrant placed on his life by the king and queen of the land.

To that injury (or disappointment) is added anger. When the untreated wound festers, an infection called anger invades. The injury and the anger multiplies with self-pity, and the person begins to feel unappreciated, mistreated, and alone in his adversity. Job found no comfort from his three friends who ran to him.

Add anger to injury, multiply by self-pity, and this is the perfect formula for depression. That formula works across the board for anyone, including Jonah. However, whereas Job's depression was God-inflicted, Jonah's depression was the result of self-inflicted injury.

God told Jonah to warn the people of Nineveh, the capital city of Assyria, of His coming wrath. The message Jonah was to preach to inhabitants was that they were to change their ways in 40 days or God would destroy them because of their wickedness. Jonah was in a city near Joppa, which was located on the coastline of the Mediterranean Sea and near Damascus and Syria. Instead of traveling northwest toward Nineveh, he ran east, boarded a ship bound for Spain.

Jonah's plan for escaping the presence of God failed. God launched a storm that wreaked havoc on the ship and the ship's mariners. Not wanting to die in the storm, the sailors unloaded all the nonessentials, and the captain found Jonah asleep below deck. Realizing that Jonah was more than likely the reason for their imperilment, the captain called for a lottery. Of course, Jonah was found guilty.

Jonah admitted that he was running from God, and he testified that God was the creator of this sea and the storm. He also added that the ship was in trouble because of him. "...*I know that for my sake this great tempest is upon you.*" (Jonah 1:12)

When Jonah advised them to throw him overboard, the sailors did not want to because they did not want to be guilty of shedding innocent blood. However, the fury of the storm made it necessary for them to do as Jonah bid, "...*and the sea ceased from her raging.*" (Jonah 1:15) God was not without a plan. He had already prepared a great fish to swallow Jonah and keep His disobedient prophet safe.

When Jonah was swallowed by this giant fish, he went down into the bottom of the mountains. The tallest mountains on earth are the ones in the sea, and most of the islands are simply the tops of those mountain peaks. Jonah felt the intense pressure of the depths, and he felt like he was dying. He likened his three-day journey in the whale to Hell. "*For as Jonas was three days and three nights in the whale's belly; so shall the Son of man be three days and three nights in the heart of the earth.*" (Matthew 12:40) Like Jonah came out of that fish, Jesus rose from the grave.

When Jonah was vomited by the fish, he left immediately for Nineveh. As soon as he arrived, he began preaching; and after one sermon, the greatest recorded revival in the history of mankind occurred! The people not only believed in God; the king commanded that every man, woman, child, and animal be clothed in sackcloth. Jonah 3:8 says, "*But let man and beast be covered with sackcloth, and cry mightily unto God: yea, let them turn every one from his evil way, and from the violence that is in their* hands." God was so impressed by the humility of the entire city that He changed His mind about His planned destruction of the whole city.

Instead of rejoicing over the salvation of an entire city, Jonah was furious. Imagine being indignant about people's being saved! In Jonah 4:11, the Bible says, "...*more than sixscore thousand persons that cannot discern between their right hand and their left hand...*" lived in the city of Nineveh. Most Bible students believe that reference means children under the age of accountability. There were at least 120,000 people in that city, and most Bible scholars believe probably 600,000 to 1,000,000 people resided in Nineveh. The Bible says it was a great city.

Jonah did not go to Nineveh to see the people saved; he wanted God to judge them and destroy them. Jonah was so upset with God that he stayed outside the city for 40 days waiting to see God wreak judgment on the people. When 40 days passed and the heathen were not destroyed, Jonah became so depressed about the situation that he wanted to die. As he was seething in the hot sun, God prepared a huge leafy gourd to shelter His angry, depressed prophet from the heat. Jonah was thrilled with the shade and relief from the sun the gourd provided.

The next day God sent a worm to kill the gourd, and the plant withered. He then sent a wind to blow away the protective leaves. Jonah "...*fainted, and wished in himself to die, and said, It is better for me to die than to live.*" (Jonah 4:8) At that point, Jonah became so depressed that he slipped to the edge of depression and wavered unsteadily toward the precipice of despair. Severe depression brings despair. Both Job and Elijah reached the point of despair. What happened in Jonah's life to take him to the brink of suicide?

1. **Jonah was an emotional extremist.** The many extremes

of Jonah are listed throughout the four chapters of the book in the Bible named after him. Jonah 1:1, 2, *"Now the word of the LORD came unto Jonah the son of Amittai, saying, Arise, go to Nineveh, that great city, and cry against it...."* Jonah was commanded to obey God and preach.

Jonah 1:3, *"But Jonah rose up to flee unto Tarshish from the presence of the LORD...."* Jonah ran from God.

Jonah 1:9, *"And he said unto them, I am an Hebrew; and I fear the LORD, the God of heaven...."* Jonah feared God, but he disobeyed Him.

Jonah 1:10, *"...Why hast thou done this? For the men knew that he fled from the presence of the LORD, because he had told them."* Jonah ran from God.

Jonah 2:1, 2, *"Then Jonah prayed unto the LORD his God out of the fish's belly, And said, I cried by reason of mine affliction unto the LORD...."* Jonah prayed for deliverance. As he ran from God, he prayed that God would save him and deliver him.

Jonah 2:9, *"But I will sacrifice unto thee with the voice of thanksgiving; I will pay that that I have vowed. Salvation is of the LORD."* Jonah said salvation is of God; he said, "Save me, God, but don't save anyone else" because he wanted the heathen to go to Hell.

Jonah 4:1, *"But it displeased Jonah exceedingly, and he was very angry."* Jonah was thoroughly unhappy, and he was very displeased.

In Jonah 4:6, *"And the LORD God prepared a gourd, and made it to come up over Jonah, that it might be a shadow over his head, to deliver him from his grief. So Jonah was exceeding glad of the gourd."* Jonah was immeasurably happy.

Twice Jonah begged to die. (Jonah 4:3, 4:8) Twice, Jonah begged to live. (Jonah 2:2, Jonah 4:6) Jonah loved the benefits; he hated the people. Jonah was capable of extreme highs—

"exceeding glad"; and he was capable of extreme lows—"exceedingly displeased." The more height a person is capable of reaching, the greater the depths he will reach. Self-inflicted depression comes when people do not get control of their emotions and get some stability. *Let your moderation be known unto all men."* (Philippians 4:5a)

The wisest man in the Bible warned people against being overly wise. He was saying the more a person knows, the more potential that person has to know things that will hurt his emotions. Some people deal constantly with unneeded depression because of self-inflicted injuries. Some of these injuries can be easily avoided.

• Some people watch every news program on every available station on the television. They are thereby learning about situations in life over which they have no control and that they cannot repair. Jonah was that kind of man; he would have watched the news reports and become even more frustrated with what was happening in Nineveh. The news of our nation has done more to depress America than any other single source. Journalists bombard our minds with knowledge and information with the hopes of getting a reaction.

• Some make the mistake of reading too many newspapers. Read the cartoons, read the front page of the sports section, and then throw away the paper.

• Some need to stop playing all their violent video games. Read and study Genesis 6 for the real reason why God sent the flood. God destroyed the world because of violence. Stop playing those violent games with realistic graphics of people being killed with machine guns and blood running all over on the television screen. It is violence, and that kind of violence upsets people emotionally.

- Some need to just take a big, deep breath and relax.

2. Jonah had misplaced loyalties. A child comes home from school with a story of being mistreated. A parent with misplaced loyalty reacts in defense of his child rather than practically and patiently seeking the truth. A child needs his parents to train him according to truth, not according to the "blood-is-thicker-than-water" motto. The teacher and the principal deserve a hearing. Have enough common decency to know that there are at least two sides to the story. When a parent misplaces his loyalty and is out of control like a mercurial Jonah, he unwisely sides with his child, leaves the church, takes his kids out of the Christian school, and starts on the path to depression. We become vulnerable to depression when we are more loyal to our children than to truth and obedience. Our children do have the capability and the propensity for sinning. It might just be that your child sinned. And even if the child did not sin, there needs to be a loyalty to the truth that supersedes a violent emotional reaction. The worst thing to do is pick up the phone after a violent reaction and tell someone who is totally unrelated to the situation about your child's mistreatment. Misplaced loyalties can bring depression.

Jonah was more loyal to his corrupt country than he was to God's righteous commands. The reason why Jonah did not want to go to Nineveh was not that he was fearful of mistreatment by the people of Nineveh. Jonah did not want to go because he hated the people of Nineveh. Because he was a prophet, he knew that one day the Assyrians would come, take ten of the twelve tribes into captivity, and totally destroy them. Assyria's future attack on the nation of Israel was the direct result of the hand of God. Jonah was far more patriotic to a corrupt nation than he was to the righteous commands of God. Jonah became depressed because of his misplaced loyalties. Self-inflicted depression comes when a person places his loyalty in some inappropriate entity. "My hope is built on nothing less—Than Jesus' blood and righteousness."

3. **Jonah was a self-serving sacrificer.** Jonah made a heroic trip to Nineveh, preached a powerful sermon, and all the people repented and got saved. His response was, "I'd rather die." People get out of sorts in churches because they are not volunteer sacrificers for Jesus Christ. Obligatory sacrifice is not true sacrifice.

Colossians 3:22 says, "...*not with eyeservice, as menpleasers; but in singleness of heart, fearing God.*" When a person serves, there is only One Whose affection and approval he should seek, and that is Christ. Looking for approval from others only brings disappointment and then depression.

Be sure that your motives are right for serving Christ because if you serve Him for His sake, you encompass yourself with a shield that keeps you from being depressed when people disapprove of you and don't appreciate you. The only real reason to serve is that you want to please the King of Kings. He is the only One you should really want to be proud of you.

Chapter Seventeen

Letting Go of the Past

"And unto the angel of the church in Sardis write; These things saith he that hath the seven Spirits of God, and the seven stars; I know thy works, that thou hast a name that thou livest, and art dead. Be watchful, and strengthen the things which remain, that are ready to die: for I have not found thy works perfect before God. Remember therefore how thou hast received and heard, and hold fast, and repent. If therefore thou shalt not watch, I will come on thee as a thief, and thou shalt not know what hour I will come upon thee. Thou hast a few names even in Sardis which have not defiled their garments; and they shall walk with me in white: for they are worthy. He that overcometh, the same shall be clothed in white raiment; and I will not blot out his name out of the book of life, but I will confess his name before my Father, and before his angels. He that hath an ear, let him hear what the Spirit saith unto the churches." (Revelation 3:1-6)

IN FEBRUARY 2001, THE Hyles family gathered around a bed in the cardiac care unit of the University of Chicago Hospital and prayed, begged, and pleaded with God; they did everything humanly possible to will the body of our beloved pastor to heal itself. We tried to will him to open the eyes that had been shut since going into surgery many hours earlier. We tried by sheer desire and willpower to force his body to live again. We anointed our beloved leader with oil and prayed for him. A watch of security guards in a waiting room several yards away prayed silently. The students at the schools he had founded were praying and pleading. Church members by the thousands were praying and pleading. Beloved friends across America and around the world by the tens and even hundreds of thousands were praying for a miracle.

However, at 9:43 a.m. on February 6, 2001, the family had to make a very difficult decision. The ventilator machine was making a raspy mechanical noise, forcing the lungs to inflate and contract. Another machine was sending an electrical charge to the heart muscle to make it pump. Other essential pieces of electronic equipment surrounded his bed. Finally, the doctor and a nurse came in. One of them touched my arm, quietly asked me to step outside, and said, "There is nothing more we can do; he is gone."

We had already decided ahead of time that we would shut off the ventilator if nothing more could be done. When the ventilator stopped its raspy breathing, we watched the blip of the heart monitor slow, go straight, and flat line. The pumps pushing fluids into the body became silent. The doctors and nurses left the room. Silence reigned.

Then came one of the most difficult times in the world to face. We had to turn from his bedside, walk out of that hospital room, and leave the body of the man who was the symbol of everything we loved. We felt as though we were abandoning our loved one at the most difficult time in his life. The emotions were so conflicting.

We were not abandoning him for he had already departed us. He was not there. We knew the soul and spirit had already escaped, but to walk away from his body still made us feel like we were abandoning him. To accept the fact that he was gone was the most difficult of decisions because we felt as long as we could be in close proximity to that body that somehow he might wake up. We stood there for a long time, sang songs, prayed, held hands, and stroked his cheek. The realization that his eyes were lifeless and that the warmth was escaping his body was heartbreaking. When we finally walked out of that room, we felt like our whole world had just evaporated.

The truth is, that hospital room no longer contained Brother Hyles; he was not confined to that cooling body. He was not there; but the fact remains that he still is very much alive! The doctors pronounced that at 9:43 he officially stopped living by their technical definition, but somewhere in that time frame, his soul and spirit departed without our noticing. He was gone; yet, he was very much alive and very happy in a very different place—finally free from earthly pain.

The specter of death looms over more than just human life. Well-meaning, good people attempt to preserve old, dilapidated buildings in an effort to cling to the corpse of the downtown heydays of yesteryears. However, sometimes the dreams of preserving the historicity of a city street are merely an effort to cling to that which has long been lifeless. To leave the past is sometimes very difficult—especially when a person must walk away from everything that seemingly embodied his security and identity.

In our early efforts to attain the proper permissions to build the new church auditorium, I met with many people who were clinging to the past glory days of Hammond. One of the men with whom I met said, "Look at these buildings; they're history. There's life in there."

I said, "Yes, they are a part of history, but there is no life in them. That body was pronounced dead many years ago. The pictures you have of those Saturday nights in Hammond when clean-cut crowds thronged the thoroughfares and the city buses were filled with busy shoppers are sweet, wonderful memories." We cannot forever cling to the deceased bodies of buildings that once lived and breathed with growth and commerce. As difficult as it may be to walk away from those empty buildings, we must.

Still, it was as difficult for those clinging to the glory days of Hammond to see buildings being razed as it was for the Hyles family to leave behind the body of their loved one in a cold hospital room. The decision was made to walk away from the past; the question that remained was **when** to walk away from the past. One of the most painful decisions every person must make in life is to recognize the past, to know he must turn away from it, then to walk away at the proper time, and to leave the past behind.

In 1959 Brother Hyles came to Hammond and became the pastor of First Baptist Church. At that time, First Baptist Church was a member of the American Baptist Convention, which was once a flourishing denomination. One year after Brother Hyles came, he lead the people of First Baptist Church to make a very difficult decision. Some people could not leave the room where the corpse of the American Baptist Denomination had ceased to breathe because that corpse seemingly held so much security and identity for them. They could not allow a young pastor to lead them to walk away from the past and take their church to the next level of growth. With the arrival of Brother Hyles came the time for First Baptist Church to walk away from that which had been holding it down and thereby release it to that which it could become. Some good, wonderful, tenderhearted, God-fearing people refused to walk away from the past.

One of the greatest causes of depression is the inability and unwillingness to walk away from the past. Those who cling to the past are forced to live a depressed life. When a person ultimately makes the decision to walk away from the past, he may feel a temporary depression which will soon pass. The Hyles family was not happy, nor were we rejoicing when we left that hospital room. We were not singing happy songs when we left. We left with tears streaming down our faces, tightly gripping our spouses and loved ones, and we walked away from that room feeling like life had just died. For a little while, we went through heaviness. Once in a while, we still sink into a heaviness, but there is life when the past is buried!

The American Baptist Convention is dead; not one growing, thriving church in fundamental Christianity is associated with that corpse. That is not a negative statement, nor is it a criticism of the American Baptist Convention; it is a statement of fact. Those who refused to say goodbye to it missed out on the greatest event that has happened in church history since the second chapter of Acts. They missed being a part of the phenomenal growth; the legendary bus ministry; the homeless ministry; the sailor ministry; the one million souls who walked the aisles of First Baptist Church under Brother Hyles' ministry; the 38 Pastors' Schools; the inception of Hammond Baptist Schools, Hyles-Anderson College, and City Baptist Schools; the rescue mission; and all the outreach ministries. They lost all these blessings because they could not walk away from the past.

Inability to leave the past is the reason a marriage struggles. It is why a family continues to struggle with the same problems over and over again. They cannot walk away from the mistakes of the past which they refuse to bury. Some are so plagued by their past failures and mistakes that they are robbing themselves of present and future successes. Past mistakes, past errors of judgment, horrific decisions that caused a person terrible loss and shame still bring that person tremendous depression today because he cannot say goodbye to the past.

1. Holding to the past cannot revive the dead; it only delays the inevitable burial. Instead of holding on to the past and constantly reliving that error of judgment, let it die and walk away. Bury it now; have a funeral service. Pull the plugs, turn off the ventilator, turn from the bedside, and walk into the future.

Marriages are condemned and plagued because the couple cannot walk out of the hospital room of the past. The ventilator machine is artificially keeping alive the dead remembrances and the reproach and the shame. Everybody involved is defiled in the present because of an inability to bury the past and step into the future.

2. Holding to the past only corrupts the present and deforms the future. You can't hang onto the past because the past begins to change as soon as life leaves. With death comes corruption. If you do not let go of the past, you bring the corruption to your present. You corrupt your relationships, and many a family is cursed because of the corruption of the past that is brought to the present. The future is deformed because you are dragging the body of death with you.

That is exactly why Paul shouted, *"O wretched man that I am! who shall deliver me from the body of this death?"* (Romans 7:24) One day Paul had a burial service, and he buried Saul of Tarsus, the murderer of Christians. Like Paul the Apostle, we must also walk away from the past, or it will corrupt the present and deform the future.

3. The spirit cannot be set free until the body dies. Past sins, past failures, and past mistakes all depress the spirit. You have a depressed spirit because in the past you committed a grievous act against the Spirit of God or against your own character. The one who lives bemoaning the past mistakes misses golden opportunities. Until that past is released, the spirit that can change the lives of many is repressed and depressed. Living with that chained body of death makes a person radiate depression and exude unhappiness. Walk away from the past; claim the Spirit that gives life!

4. **The only way the old can live again is to be reborn.** Right now Brother Hyles is still alive: he is spiritually reborn in Heaven. He is also reborn in our spirits. As we learned from him, loved him, and walked with him while he walked among us, we caught his spirit and we learned to live and to love. He still lives because those of us who loved him will continue the legacy and carry it on. We will carry on with what he taught us. I am going to continue what he taught me. We will teach like he taught. We will love like he loved. We will give like he gave. We have made the decision to have a little bit of the spirit of Jack Hyles reborn within us. In so doing, we have said goodbye to the past and are headed toward the future!

Chapter Eighteen

The Depressing
Giant of Unbelief

"*And they went and came to Moses, and to Aaron, and to all the congregation of the children of Israel, unto the wilderness of Paran, to Kadesh; and brought back word unto them, and unto all the congregation, and shewed them the fruit of the land. And they told him, and said, We came unto the land whither thou sentest us, and surely it floweth with milk and honey; and this is the fruit of it. Nevertheless the people be strong that dwell in the land, and the cities are walled, and very great: and moreover we saw the children of Anak there. The Amalekites dwell in the land of the south: and the Hittites, and the Jebusites, and the Amorites, dwell in the mountains: and the Canaanites dwell by the sea, and by the coast of Jordan. And Caleb stilled the people before Moses, and said, Let us go up at once, and possess it; for we are well able to overcome it. But the men that went up with him said, We be not able to go up against the people; for they are stronger than we. And they brought up an evil report of the land which they had searched unto the children of Israel, saying, The land, through which we have gone to search it, is a land that eateth up the inhabitants thereof; and all the people that we saw in it are men of a great stature. And there we saw the giants, the sons of Anak, which come of the giants: and we were in our own sight as grasshoppers, and so we were in their sight. And all the congregation lifted up their voice, and cried; and the people wept that night. And all the children of Israel murmured against Moses and against Aaron: and the whole congregation said unto them, Would God that we had died in the land of Egypt! or would God we had died in this wilderness! And wherefore hath the LORD brought us unto this land, to fall by the sword, that our wives and our children should be a prey? were it not better for us to return into Egypt?"* (Numbers 13:26-14:3)

IN THE DESERTS OF modern-day Saudi Arabia, a small band of warriors under the leadership of Moses was about to engage the enemy—the giants of Canaan. Brother Hyles often said that Moses was perhaps the greatest leader in history and certainly the greatest leader in the Old Testament and Bible history. Moses was leading 3.5 million people in the wilderness—not farmland. His people were taking their flocks of sheep and herds of cattle with them. There were no water, no ready food supply, no farms, no stores or markets, no sanitation treatment plants, no irrigation ditches, no hospitals—nothing but wilderness. With Moses at the helm, they crossed the Red Sea, a vast, very deep body of water. God performed a miracle, and 3.5 million Jews crossed on dry ground between solid walls of water, and the Egyptian army was devoured by the waves the next morning.

As Moses led them on what could have been an eleven-day journey, they stopped to receive the Ten Commandments, the laws of God. They received a new constitution and appointed themselves as a new nation—the nation of Israel. God wanted them to learn some policies, as well as to learn everything from how to care for waste material in the desert, to how to handle the food and supplies, to how to set in motion the sacrifice system that God had implemented. Finally, 16 months after leaving Egypt, the Israelites were at the border of the Promised Land, the place where they had longed to be. For 200 years while serving as slaves in Egypt, they had listened to the stories of Abraham, Isaac, Jacob, and Joseph. Finally, they were returning to the homeland of their ancestors! What a wonderful opportunity was at their fingertips!

At the border of this new homeland, Moses appointed 12 spies, one man from each of the 12 tribes of Israel, to infiltrate the region, to assess the strength of the people, to locate the cities, and to plot some routes into the land. The men entered the land when the harvest of grapes was at its peak. In fact, two men returned carrying one cluster of grapes on a pole. The men spied out a great land of plenty—a land of milk and honey. The Promised Land was a land of riches, wealth, and abundance; after spending six months in a barren desert, any change of scenery would have been good.

The 12 spies returned after 40 days of searching the land. Imagine the excitement of the children of Israel as they gathered around the spies to hear their report to Moses. However, as ten of the spies began their report, shock and disappointment crept over the assembly as they addressed the impossibility of crossing the Canaanland boundaries, marching into the land, and conquering the Amalekites, the Amorites, the Hittites, the Hivites, and the Canaanites.

Caleb was stunned by the ten spies' cowardly report. He knew the promises of God and tried to encourage the people to continue forward and take what God had already given to them. *"And Caleb stilled the people before Moses, and said, Let us go up at once, and possess it; for we are well able to overcome it."* (Numbers 13:30)

The ten spies stopped Caleb from rallying the people, and they continued their evil report of the land with a description of "...*giants, the sons of Anak, which come of the giants: and we were in our own sight as grasshoppers, and so we were in their sight.*" (Numbers 13:33) Ten spies saw the Promised Land as an unconquerable land, and their negative report turned the hearts of the people toward the past. "...*Would God that we had died in the land of Egypt!*" (Numbers 14:2)

The people decided to elect a captain to lead them back to Egypt's bondage. They were more ready to go back into slavery, rather than to face the freedom God had for them. These Israelites had just been released from horrible conditions in Egypt. Many were beaten by the whips of the Egyptians who despised them; they were nothing more than property to be bought and sold.

In their depression, they honestly felt that going back to the abuse of the Egyptians far outweighed possessing the Promised Land. Caleb could not understand how it could possibly be better to face the horrific conditions of slavery in Egypt when freedom was just a few steps away. He had finally washed Egypt's defilement and filth from his own body and was ready to taste the sweetness of freedom. He could not believe or understand why his fellow countrymen were so ready to put themselves once again into willful bondage to be abused, tortured, and murdered.

The nation of Israel did not enter Canaanland because of the negative reaction of the crowd. As a result, God decided to let them wander in the desert wilderness for 40 years—one year for each of the 40 days the spies canvassed the land. Six hundred five thousand soldiers died in wilderness over the next forty years. Only two men lived—Caleb and Joshua. Women and children under 20 years of age also survived God's terrible judgment.

Hebrews 3:19–4:1 tells why the children of Israel did not enter the Promised Land: *"So we see that they could not enter in because of **unbelief**. Let us therefore fear, lest, a promise being left us of entering into his rest, any of you should seem to come short of it."* Six hundred five thousand trained soldiers died over the next forty years because of one word—unbelief.

Unbelief underestimates a person's own abilities. Upon hearing the negative reports, the nation of Israel said, "We cannot! We are as grasshoppers in their sight." Unbelief always underestimates a person's abilities. The focus turns to **me**; I am thinking too much about my ability or lack of it. As soon as a person starts thinking about whether or not he is able, he will automatically start thinking about his weaknesses. Excuses are nothing more than unbelief which says, "I would rather go back into slavery than enter my promised land."

Unbelief overestimates the enemy's abilities. As unbelief rises in our nation, so does the emphasis on the occult, Satanism, and witchcraft. The rise of Satanism and occultism is the direct result of the unbelief of Christians. When unbelief takes over, blaming comes into play.

This business of the "the Devil made me do it" is nonsense. A person's unbelief "made him do it." The Devil receives far too much credit for what is wrong in America. Satan was de-fanged and declawed at Calvary, and the only power he possesses is the power to frighten us. Our unbelief is nothing more than fearing that Satan may harm us, but he has no power other than what we give him.

Christians need to focus their attention on the Lord Jesus Christ and realize that the Devil is a defeated enemy. The Bible tells us, *"…greater is he that is in you, than he that is in the world."* (I John 4:4) *"I can do all things through Christ which strengtheneth me."* (Philippians 4:13) If the children of Israel had focused their attention on Caleb, their future would have been drastically different!

Unbelief ignores the promises of God. The ten spies who felt the land could not be conquered said, *"And they brought up an evil report of the land which they had searched unto the children of Israel, saying, The land, through which we have gone to search it, is a land that eateth up the inhabitants thereof...."* (Numbers 13:32) Caleb had a ready answer for their fearfulness. *"Only rebel not ye against the LORD, neither fear ye the people of the land; for they are bread for us: their defence is departed from them, and the LORD is with us: fear them not."* (Numbers 14:9) Caleb saw the inhabitants of the land as a loaf of bread. Because the Lord was on their side, the enemy would be torn apart like pieces of bread and scattered across a lawn to feed the birds.

A person's unbelief magnifies his inability, magnifies his enemy's ability, and diminishes God's ability. God gets smaller, the problems get bigger, the enemy looms larger, and the unbelieving one becomes weaker.

Too many people serve a little tiny god when in fact we have Jehovah God on our side! We have the promises of His Book at our fingertips. We have the Spirit of the living God living inside of us. *"If God be for us, who can be against us?"* (Romans 8:31b)

Forty years later, Caleb and Joshua entered the Promised Land because they believed God. Caleb was commended by God for his belief. *"But my servant Caleb, because he had another spirit with him, and hath followed me fully...."* (Numbers 14:24) Caleb's *another spirit* means "a following spirit." Caleb possessed a spirit that was willing to follow. God is not looking for leaders; He is looking for followers. He is not looking for kings; He is looking for servants.

Caleb possessed a spirit different from the murmuring and complaining spirit of the children of Israel. When the children of Israel were hungry and thirsty in the wilderness, more than likely Caleb was hungry and thirsty too. One way to arouse the ire and wrath of God was murmuring and complaining—something of which the children of Israel were often guilty.

Caleb was dominated by a spirit different from the rebellious spirit of Korah, Dathan, and Abiram. Their spirit of rebellion cost them and their families the Promised Land; instead, they suffered the wrath of God when the earth split, and they went straight to Hell.

Caleb was consumed by a spirit different from the spirit of the fringe crowd who lived on the edge and often became victims. In the center of the nation of Israel was the tabernacle of God. The Levites, led by Aaron, lived there. As the leader, Moses stayed in the center. However, the people who lived on the fringe often fell victim to marauding bands of robbers. Caleb wanted to be in the thick of serving the Lord. He jumped in head first, planted both feet, and buried himself in the will of God.

Caleb had a spirit different from the spirit of those who looked back at the past. He left the whips and chains of slavery behind. Caleb knew what was ahead had to be much better than what was behind. The worst thing that Christianity can offer is better than anything good the world could offer. Caleb knew facing a giant in the will of God was far better than facing certain slavery behind him.

Caleb had a spirit different from those filled with a fearful spirit. The Israelites wanted to stay on the easy side of Jordan rather than fight the Canaanites. Three of the tribes said they had come far enough. They refused to cross Jordan because they had crossed one body of water too many. Caleb wanted to be in the center of the battle.

Caleb possessed another spirit; he didn't understand the unbelief and depression of those who cried, "...*would God we had died in this wilderness!*" God gave His people their wish; they died in the wilderness. He spared only Joshua and Caleb and women and children under 20 years of age. But to Caleb He gave a promise: "*But my servant Caleb, because had another spirit with him, and hath followed me fully, him will I bring into the land whereinto he went; and his seed shall possess it.*" (Numbers 14:24)

CHAPTER NINETEEN

LIFE IS A CHOICE

"But I rejoiced in the Lord greatly, that now at the last your care of me hath flourished again; wherein ye were also careful, but ye lacked opportunity. Not that I speak in respect of want: for I have learned, in whatsoever state I am, therewith to be content. I know both how to be abased, and I know how to abound: every where and in all things I am instructed both to be full and to be hungry, both to abound and to suffer need. I can do all things through Christ which strengtheneth me." (Philippians 4:10-13)

"For he that will love life, and see good days, let him refrain his tongue from evil, and his lips that they speak no guile: Let him eschew evil, and do good; let him seek peace, and ensue it. For the eyes of the Lord are over the righteous, and his ears are open unto their prayers: but the face of the Lord is against them that do evil. And who is he that will harm you, if ye be followers of that which is good? But and if ye suffer for righteousness' sake, happy are ye: and be not afraid of their terror, neither be troubled." (I Peter 3:10-14)

GOD HAS GRANTED TO every human being the miracle of life. Whether a person's life ends today or tomorrow or continues for many more years, the bottom line is that for however long a person has to enjoy the adventure of living in God's kingdom on this earth, he has been privileged to have this intangible called life.

1. **Every human being has been granted a tremendous opportunity and privilege of being alive and being aware of it.** God made this sphere we call earth the only place in the universe that is inhabitable by human beings. Because He made it for our habitation, all the ingredients were in exactly the right percentages and right proportions. A little over 6,000 years ago, it occurred to God (if anything has ever occurred to God), to create human beings.

God made a limited number of human beings. Everyone who happens to be breathing His air, living on His earth, enjoying all His blessings of life, as well as enduring all the struggles that come with life, obviously has been granted the privilege of being alive. Realizing the alternative is never to have been born, I believe I would rather suffer the negative ingredients of life than to have never been born at all! It is the profoundest of honors to be given the privilege to be alive, to enjoy living, and to be aware of the privilege of life.

The first thing I do when I wake up is thank God that I'm alive. I say, "Good morning, Lord. I thank You that I'm alive. I thank You for life and the privilege to be alive, and I thank You for the air I breathe. I thank You that I have the mental awareness to know that I am alive, and that there is a God Who has granted me this special privilege." Life is a daily adventure, and I start each day thanking God for the things He does for me.

As I prepare for the day, I thank God for the hot water I enjoy using on cold winter mornings. I think of the times Brother Hyles told of knocking ice off the water bucket, pumping more water, and carrying it inside. He then carried in the wood to feed the fire to heat the water. When the water was heated and poured into the #2 tub, he was the last to use the water. I thank God that all I have to do is flip a lever and enjoy the hot water that pours from a faucet. Thank God for hot running water!

Some people have go to Great America or Disney World before they can enjoy life; I just need hot water running over my head. I thank God for indoor plumbing; there is no path to a small building in my backyard. I thank God for electric lights. People who live in third-world countries would love to have electric lights at the flip of a switch. I thank God for the furnace that blows hot air to keep me warm in the winter and for the cool air of the air conditioning in the summer. I thank God for the washing machine and dryer that my wife uses to do the laundry. I appreciate the little things about life. We've been granted a great privilege to live.

2. **Life does consist, however, of both positive and negative events.** Nobody has all positives, and likewise, nobody has all negatives. Enjoyable events or dreaded events or anticipated events come into every person's life.

3. **These events come to us without choice on our part, but according to the divine mind of God.** These events are not planned by the individual into whose life they come, nor are they were voted on by him; they are appointed and chosen by the divine mind of God. In Job 2:10, Job said to his wife, "...*What? shall we receive good at the hand of God, and shall we not receive evil?*" Job was saying that God gave them good things, and God also gave them hurtful events in their lives. Job did not have a choice about the catastrophic events that entered his life. God chooses the events that enter our lives.

For some, God's choices of events are positive. For instance, some have the satisfaction of rearing good, godly children. Some couples enjoy an excellent, unparalleled marriage. On the other hand, He chooses some to endure negative events. A man in our church was married to and lived with a severely handicapped wife for 17 years. Many had an idea of the kind of struggles that couple endured, but no one could possibly understand the degree of the struggle he experienced. That man said, "After 17 years of that kind of struggle, it taught me to be mighty thankful for all the good things I have in life." To another, the diagnosis of a dread disease becomes the unexpected event of life. For Marlene Evans, it was not, "Why me, Lord?" it was "Why not me?"

4. **I must accept the fact that both the positive and negative ingredients make up my life.** Those ingredients have been uniquely designed by the hand of God for each person. God makes the choices.

The death of a family member is not a choice anyone can make. God alone makes the choice.

An unexpected medical test is prescribed. Along with the prescription comes the upheaval of wondering, fear, pain, possible surgery, more pain, bills…and then comes the answer to the prayer—"benign." The process to the diagnosis was no fun, but what a wonderful word benign is!

Job downsizing and pay cuts enter the arena of another's life. Four weeks of paid vacation suddenly shrinks to two weeks of unpaid vacation. That employee certainly had no choice in the matter; it is doubtful that the company asked for his opinion. The events of life continue to transpire, and we must accept the fact that both the positive and negative ingredients are a part of life.

5. **I must not concern myself with what event will be drawn out next; that is God's business.** When the holocaust of

trials hit, many think, "What's next?!" To be sure, nothing is enjoyable about the negative events of life. However, living in fear of the future means we cannot live life in the present. Today is the only day we have to live. We cannot live tomorrow, nor can we relive yesterday. We can only live today. We cannot waste today wondering about yesterday or tomorrow. Instead, we need to let life come to us; we cannot race ahead of it.

6. **Each event of life forces a response out of me.** The person who experiences an event reaches inside of his heart and pulls out a response. Many responses reside in a person's heart: praise, trust, thanksgiving, criticism, complaining, frustration, anger, self-pity, comforting others. Every event that a person faces forces one of these kinds of responses.

For instance, a couple enjoys the blessing of having their children love and serve God. That event of life should elicit praise and thanksgiving. Each event of life forces a response out of the recipient. As previously stated, he does not have a choice in the event; he only has a choice in his response. Lodged deep inside every person's heart are responses he has the choice to make.

When a job downsizing takes place, a natural response would be criticism of unwise management. On the other hand, a proper response might be praise for the many years the job supported your family.

As difficult as it may seem, the proper response when a negative event comes in life is to turn to God and ask, "Lord, what do You not want me to do?" Let Christ take away the negative options of criticism, complaining, and suchlike.

We did not have the option to choose life. We could not choose the events of life. We were not allowed to choose the order in which the events of life came. We could not choose whether the events would be positive or negative. The only choice we have in all of life is our response to the events God allows in our lives. We must discard all of our options and give Him that choice too!

> "'Tis so sweet to trust in Jesus,
> Just to take Him at His Word;
> Just to rest upon His promise;
> Just to know, 'Thus saith the Lord.'
> Jesus, Jesus, how I trust Him!..."